The Heretical Imperative

Peter L. Berger is Professor of Sociology at Rutgers University and is the author of *A Rumor of Angels*, *Sacred Canopy*, *Invitation to Sociology*, and *Pyramids of Sacrifice*, among other books.

THE
Heretical Imperative

CONTEMPORARY POSSIBILITIES OF RELIGIOUS AFFIRMATION

Peter L. Berger

1979
ANCHOR PRESS/DOUBLEDAY
GARDEN CITY, NEW YORK

The Anchor Books edition is the first publication of *The Heretical Imperative*.

Anchor Books edition: 1979

ISBN: 0-385-14286-2
Library of Congress Catalog Card Number 78–20106

Contents

PREFACE   ix

1   *Modernity as the Universalization of Heresy*   1

    The Modern Situation   3

    From Fate to Choice   11

    A Plurality of Worldviews   17

    A Very Nervous Prometheus   22

    The Heretical Imperative   26

2   *Religion: Experience, Tradition, Reflection*   32

    Many Realities   36

    Religion as Experience   41

    Religion as Tradition   46

    Once More: The Modern Situation   54

    Assorted Protestant Miseries   56

    Three Options for Religious Thought   60

3   *The Deductive Possibility:*
    Reaffirming Tradition   66

The Case of Protestant Neo-orthodoxy   68

"A Flake-like Thing on the Face of the Wilderness"   74

Critique of Leaping   79

Reflecting on Thunder   87

4 *The Reductive Possibility:*
   Modernizing Tradition   95

Bargaining with Modernity   98

Bargaining Away "Mythology"   101

A Translation Model   110

Critique of the Model   117

Man as Symbolizer and as Symbol   121

5 *The Inductive Possibility:*
   From Tradition to Experience   125

Back to Schleiermacher   127

An Inductive Model   135

Criticisms of the Model   139

The Quest for Certainty and Its Frustrations   145

In Defense of Mellowness   153

6 *Between Jerusalem and Benares:*
   The Coming Contestation of Religions   157

"The Dharma Is Going West"   158

Contents

The Divine in Confrontation and Interiority   168

While Waiting for the Dark Drums of God   181

NOTES   191

INDEX   209

Preface

Autobiographical discursions in the preface to a book typically indicate that the author takes himself too seriously. This is a sign that he is guilty not only of the sin of vanity but of a deficient sense of humor (which is probably a more grievous sin than vanity). Yet if an author has been humorless enough, for better or for worse, to have written more than one book, his readers will understandably want to know how a new book fits in with previous ones. For this reason, and (I hope) for this reason only, I will allow myself some autobiographical or, so to speak, "autobibliographical" comments here.

It is almost exactly ten years since I worked on my last book on religion. This book was *A Rumor of Angels: Modern Society and the Rediscovery of the Supernatural* (Garden City, N.Y.: Doubleday, 1969). The present book deliberately takes up the argument at the point where the earlier book left it—to wit, at the contention that theological thought should follow an inductive approach. By this latter term I meant an approach that begins with ordinary human experience, explores the "signals of transcendence" to be found in it, and moves on from there to religious affirmations about the nature of reality. I have in no way changed my mind about this. Also, the present book is similar to *Rumor of Angels* in that it begins with analyses of the contemporary situation by using the intellectual tools of the sociology of knowledge and then, deliberately, crosses the boundary between "value-free" social science and highly evaluative theological propositions. But the present book is different from *Rumor of Angels* both in purpose and in scope. The purpose of the earlier book was to criticize the manner in which modern secular thought has sought to invalidate the reality of a religious view of the world. It employed the sociology of knowledge "to relativize the relativizers." Yet, in doing this, its focus remained on that ordinary human experience that is equally available to the village atheist and the village saint. In other words, in *Rumor of Angels* I tried to break through the assumptions of modern secularism from within. The present book shifts the focus to religious experience proper, with the purpose of exploring the applicability of an inductive approach there. This has also entailed a considerably broader scope.

For the last ten years most of my work as a sociologist has not directly dealt with religion. I have worked mostly on the theory of modernization and on problems of Third World development, and, in connection with these interests, on the uses of sociological perspectives in public policy. But my rather massive confrontation with Third World realities has made for a change in my understanding of the contemporary religious situation. Only now, in retrospect, is it clear to me how parochial my work on religion in the 1960s had been—parochial quite simply in the sense that its focus was virtually exclusively on the fate of religion in the Western world. This has implications for a number of sociological topics, notably the question of secularization. As will be clear from what follows here, there have also been theological implications for me. My understanding of "ecumenicity" has expanded very greatly. This would not be very interesting in itself but for the fact that I have become convinced that such expansion is very salutary and much to be recommended to anyone doing Christian theology today; the same recommendation holds for those in other traditions who intend to reflect systematically about religious matters today.

While the logic of the argument in this book necessitates discussions of quite varied topics, the main line of argumentation is quite simple. It is my position that modernity has plunged religion into a very specific crisis, characterized by secularity, to be sure, but characterized more importantly by pluralism. In the pluralistic situation, for reasons that are readily visible to historical and social-scientific observation, the authority of all religious traditions tends to be undermined. In this situation there are three major options, or "possibilities," for those who would maintain the tradition: They can reaffirm the authority of the tradition in defiance of the challenges to it; they can try to secularize the tradition; they can try to uncover and retrieve the experiences embodied in the tradition. For reasons spelled out in some detail, I call these three options, respectively, those of deduction, reduction, and induction. That much is a descriptive exercise, within the framework of the sociology of knowledge. I further argue, however, that only the third option, that of the inductive approach, is finally viable. I further contend that the contestation between the major world religions, particularly between the traditions emanating from the religious history of western Asia and the traditions given birth on the Indian subcontinent, should be a centrally important theme for theology and religious thought in the future.

Almost all of this argument can be made without presupposing any particular faith commitment. I have tried to argue throughout this book in a way that appeals to reasonable men of any tradition; I address myself to specifically Christian concerns only on the last few pages, and I signal clearly when I do

this. The fact that the cases of the three options discussed in
the book all come from the history of Protestant theology in no
way presupposes a Protestant commitment on the part of author or reader; I argue that Protestantism is very instructive because it has confronted modernity for the longest time and in
the most intense way; non-Protestants and non-Christians have
much to learn from this example (and not necessarily in positive ways only). Still, I have no motive to disguise the fact that
my own faith commitment is unambiguously (and, I daresay,
irrevocably) Christian. What is more, my embrace of an inductive approach in religious thought places me unmistakably
within one particular stream in the history of ideas—that of
Protestant theological liberalism, in the line of Friedrich
Schleiermacher. I have understood my theological "location" in
this way since the early 1960s; it has now become clearer, perhaps sharper. In any case, I admit it without hesitation or em-
barrassment.

In urging an inductive approach, then, I have two different
audiences in mind here. First, and more broadly, I would like
to address myself to anyone thinking seriously about religion
today; and to this audience I would like to say that such an inductive approach offers new opportunities of understanding the
religious phenomenon in a comprehensively cross-cultural way.
Second, I also would like to speak to anyone concerned with
the impasse of contemporary Christian thought. This impasse,
I believe, is the result of the sterile antithesis of neo-orthodoxy
and secularism (both appearing in different versions) that still
seems to dominate the Christian theological scene, at least in
this country. It is my belief that the time has come for a reso-
lute turning away from this antithesis and for a turning back to
the problems and methods (not necessarily the answers) of
classical theological liberalism. *There,* I feel sure, is the way out
of the present impasse.

I have the impression that to take such a position is not to play the role of one crying in the wilderness (I have no sense of mission that would make such a role plausible to myself). It seems to me that there are quite a few people whose thinking is veering in more or less this direction. I'm less clear that many of these people are to be found in the ranks of what some call "professional theologians." I still marvel that there are individuals who employ this phrase without intending irony, but that is another story. In any case, I'm very conscious of the fact that I'm here addressing theological problems without any kind of theological accreditation, and I'm enough of a sociologist to be aware of the risk of this. "Professional theologians," I have discovered, react to outsiders venturing into their staked-out preserve pretty much as other professionals react to lay initiatives—or, for that matter, as labor functionaries in a closed shop react to anyone without a union card. I readily concede my lack of a formal theological education, and I stipulate that I might have avoided some errors or shortcomings in my thinking about religion if I had benefited from such an education. *Tant pis.* One does what one can do. What the "professional theologians" have done of late is not so inspiring that we unaccredited types must feel constrained to stand watching in awed silence. Moreover, my feelings on this matter are still quite Lutheran; I believe that the priesthood of all believers also has an intellectual dimension.

One more "autobibliographical" observation: I was one of the individuals associated with the so-called Hartford Appeal. This document, which spurred a considerable controversy, was widely perceived as a statement of theological conservatism; consequently, the position I take in the present book may surprise some who perceived the Hartford Appeal in this way. Let me assure them that no change of mind on my part is involved in this either. For one thing, the perception of the Hart-

ford Appeal as a conservative manifesto was mistaken to begin
with; the notion that its authors were bent on hunting heretics
was a gross misunderstanding, largely based on the manner in
which the event was reported in the press. The Hartford Appeal was directed not against theological liberalism nor against
the political "left" but only against the intellectual capitulation
to secularism; it just so happens that today this capitulation
frequently takes the form of identifying the Christian message
with this or that left-of-center agenda; tomorrow, if the ideological mood of the American intelligentsia should change, the
very words of the Hartford document could be directed just as
well against a right-wing agenda marketed under a Christian
label. As far as my own participation in the Hartford Appeal
was concerned, I was probably the left-most member of the
group *theologically* (this, of course, does not mean that I was to
the left of the others *politically*). This was clear at the time to
anyone who bothered to inquire. As I put it then to one such
inquirer, I was not concerned with a return to the tradition but
with a return to the *struggle* with the tradition; such struggling,
I thought then and think now, is made meaningless if the tradition itself is secularized. I hope that the present book will clarify in what way I understand my position as being *neither* "reactionary" *nor* "revolutionary."

This is a book about religious thought, or theology—not
about faith but about the manner in which one may reflect
about faith. In other words, its purpose is intellectual, not
devotional or inspirational. I think it is important to stress this.
Intellectuals always tend to think that the history of the world
is the history of ideas; when theologians make this mistake, the
whole character of the religious phenomenon is distorted. Anyone engaged in a religious quest strives toward affirmation—
that is, toward an attitude in which he can say, "This I believe." For the intellectual, alas, this striving is hedged in by

more complex "possibilities" and "impossibilities." It is salutary (in the most literal sense of the word) to keep in mind that, in that *raison du coeur* on which all religious affirmations are finally based, the intellectual is not more privileged by even an iota than any other human being.

The conceptualization in chapter 2 was extensively discussed with Hansfried Kellner, to whom I am very much indebted for helping to clarify these issues in my own mind.

I wish to express my gratitude to the Exxon Education Foundation and particularly to its president, Robert Payton, for a grant allowing me to take a leave from teaching for one semester, and to Rutgers University for giving me such leave.

Loretta Barrett, my editor at Doubleday, has been most supportive all along, and I want to acknowledge this support very gratefully indeed.

P.L.B.

The Heretical Imperative

1

Modernity as the Universalization of Heresy

THE NATIONAL AIRLINE of Indonesia calls itself by the name of Garuda, the mythological bird of the Ramayana. The name, which is emblazoned on its airplanes, is appropriate. The traveler flying over the Indonesian archipelago with its myriad islands may well feel himself to be borne on the wings of the original Garuda. Which makes him too a quasi-mythological being, a god perhaps, or at least a demigod, soaring through the sky with unimaginable speed and served by machines of unimaginable power. Down below are the mere mortals, in their small villages and fields. They look up and they watch the gods fly by. Occasionally the traveler will touch down among them, but even then he rarely mingles with them. He has important business in the big cities. Or he may stay a weekend on Bali, once called the island of the gods, during which he can easily spend the equivalent of the annual per capita income of Indonesia.

The jet traveler in the Third World is a pretty good meta-

phor of modernity. He moves on the same planet as those villagers, and yet he moves in an altogether different world. His
space is measured in thousands of miles, theirs by the distance
a bullock cart can go. His time is expressed in the controlled
precision of airline schedules, theirs by the seasons of nature
and of the human body. He moves with breathtaking speed;
they move in the slow rhythms set long ago by tradition. His
life hurls itself into an open future; theirs moves in careful connection with the ancestral past. He has vast power, physical as
well as social, more or less at his command; they have very little of either. And, while he is not a god in that he is mortal, his
life-span will very likely be much longer than theirs. Seen in
the perspective of such villagers, modernity is the advent of a
new world of mythological potency. Modernization, then, is
the juxtaposition of this new world over the old worlds of traditional man—a cataclysmic and unprecedented event in human
history.

But the jet traveler differs from the villager in another very
important way. It is not only that he is so much more privileged and powerful. It is also that he has so *many more choices.*
In that too, of course, gods and demigods used to differ from
mere mortals. The jet traveler carries these choices on his person in symbolic form. He can change his air ticket and fly to
Singapore instead of Manila. He can convert his travelers'
checks into this currency or that. His passport and his credit
card open a multiplicity of doors. All these travel choices, however, represent only a small slice of an enormously larger array
of choices that are part of the taken-for-granted fabric of modern life. To be sure, a Javanese villager also makes choices, and,
anthropologically speaking, the capacity to choose is intrinsic
to human being. Also to be sure, not all modern men have the
same range of choices; thus an upper-middle-class New Yorker
may choose to have his vacation in Asia, while his working-class

neighbor chooses to get on a bus and visit his cousin in Boston. Still, compared to anyone in a premodern society, both have a range of choices which, for most of history, would have been in the realm of mythological fantasy—choices of occupation, of place of residence, of marriage, of the number of one's children, in the manner of passing one's leisure time, in the acquisition of material goods. All these are choices, and very important ones to most people, in the external arrangements of life. But there are other choices too, choices that deeply touch the inner world of individuals—choices of what is now commonly called "life-style," moral and ideological choices, and, last but not least, religious choices.

The Modern Situation

Modernity as a near-inconceivable expansion of the area of human life open to choices—that is the central theme of this book; or, rather, the central theme is the elaboration of the implications of this situation for religion. This theme, needless to say, cannot be argued at the hand of metaphors, however apt they may be. It must be elaborated systematically; in the course of such elaboration, a certain painstaking quality will at times be unavoidable.

Marion Levy has rather pithily defined the measure of modernization as "the ratio of inanimate to animate sources of power."[1] One may not be altogether satisfied with this definition (and, incidentally, Levy has elaborated on it in enormous detail in a number of books), but it has the merit of pointing clearly to two aspects of the matter: One, that modernity (which, within the context of this definition, would be a situation in which a *high* ratio of inanimate to animate sources of power prevails) is not an either/or affair but rather comes in

different degrees. And, two, that the essential factor in the
process of modernization, and *ipso facto* the core of modernity
(which is the product of the modernization process), is technological. Both of these aspects are very important. Historians, for
example, always like to point out to social scientists that this or
the other phenomenon in the contemporary world has its paral-
lel in previous periods of history. It is, indeed, intellectually salutary to be aware of historical precedents and even to recognize
that one's own situation is not altogether unheard-of in some
of its characteristics. But at the same time one must not allow
oneself to be trapped into a perspective in which there is nothing ever new in history—in which, in the last resort, no changes
can be perceived. Levy's way of defining modernization makes
one look upon it, so to speak, in a statistical manner: Modernity is an aggregate of traits; these traits appear in history in
different frequency distributions. Also, although these traits
cover a wide range of human concerns (economic, political, social, and indeed psychological), the prime causal force that
aggregates them is technological. In other words, the juxtaposition of airplane and bullock cart in the previous metaphor is
not a gratuitous one.

If one follows a phenomenon far enough back in time, one
invariably comes on a variety of causal factors. It follows that
what appears as a prime causal force in one period of history
was itself the product of other causes, some of them possibly of
a very different character. Thus the technology that has transformed the conditions of human life for the last few centuries
did not fall from heaven at the beginning of the era now called
modern. It has often been asked why it was in Europe at a particular moment that the scientific knowledge that had been
"lying around" for centuries was, almost suddenly, transmuted
into a technological revolution. Why not in ancient Greece?
Or, for that matter, in India or China? Needless to say, there

are different theories about this. These cannot be pursued here. Suffice it to say that there is no intention here of assuming some sort of technological determinism. On the contrary, it is stipulated that the technological revolution of recent history must be understood as the result of a confluence of multiple and heterogeneous causes. Thus modernity, in the form known today, was *also* caused by other specifically European phenomena—such as the capitalist market economy, the bureaucratic nation-state, the pluralistic metropolis, and the complex ideological configurations produced by the Renaissance and the Reformation. Nevertheless, the one singly most important transforming force was then, at the beginning, and continues today to be technology.

Human life and thought is always situated in history. One may then say that anyone living and thinking today is *in the situation of modernity*; depending on the country or societal sector at issue, one may modify this by saying that one lives and thinks in a situation characterized by this or that degree of modernization. This may at first appear as a banal statement, but its implications are not banal at all. What needs to be clarified is the notion of *situation*. It means, first of all, that an individual's existence takes place under certain external conditions—in this case, under the conditions brought about by a certain technology, certain economic and political arrangements, and so forth. But it also means that there is an internalization of at least some of these conditions—in this case, conditions that can be summed up by saying that a contemporary individual finds himself afflicted or blessed by the aggregate of psychological and cognitive structures commonly called *modern consciousness*. Put differently, the situation of contemporary life and thought is shaped not only by the external forces of modernity but by the forces of modern consciousness shaping the inner world of individuals. One of the most important areas of analysis is precisely this relation between the external and the internal aspects of modernity.[2]

Such a relation eminently prevails in the case of technology. Thus, for example, an individual in contemporary America is in a situation in which he frequently communicates with others by telephone. The telephone, in the most obvious way, is an external fact in the individual's life; indeed, it is a material fact, embodied in innumerable physical objects, one or more of which may clutter up the individual's house. Equally obviously, this external fact shapes many aspects of the individual's everyday life. Thus he can utilize his telephone, and the enormously complicated and powerful machinery to which it is linked (including underwater cables between continents and communications satellites orbiting the earth) to carry on a trivial conversation with a friend vacationing in Indonesia. But that is not the whole story. An individual who uses the telephone must know how to handle this particular piece of machinery. This is a skill, which after a while becomes a habit—an external habit, a bit of learned behavior. But the use of the telephone also means learning certain ways of thinking—internal habits, as it were. It means to think in numbers, to absorb a considerably complex framework of cognitive abstractions (such as the network of area codes covering North America), to have some notion of what could go wrong with the machinery (even if one must call on an expert for repairs). Anyone who has ever used the telephone in a Third World country knows that none of these things can be taken for granted. But there is more yet. To use the telephone habitually also means to learn a specific style of dealing with others—a style marked by impersonality, precision, and (at least in this country) a certain superficial civility. The key question is this: Do these internal habits *carry over* into other areas of life, such as nontelephonic relations with other persons? The answer is almost certainly yes. The problem is: Just how, and to what extent?

The example of the telephone can be replicated over the whole spectrum of the technological apparatus of contemporary life. In consequence, the question can be enormously enlarged: Does contemporary technological consciousness carry over into other areas of life? Put differently: Does contemporary man have a technological mentality that corresponds to the technological forces that shape his life externally? Again, the answer is almost certainly yes. The problem of the quality and the degree of this correspondence is far from solved. *Mutatis mutandis*, similar questions may be asked with regard to the other external facets of modernity: Is there a capitalist mentality corresponding to the capitalist market economy? Is there a bureaucratic mind corresponding to bureaucratic institutions? And so on.

Needless to say, the details of this vast problem are beyond the scope of this book. The point of the foregoing considerations is simply to bring out a simple but exceedingly important empirical fact: *Modern consciousness is part and parcel of the situation in which the contemporary individual finds himself*. Put differently, anyone today is not only situated in the modern world but is also situated within the structures of modern consciousness. Thus modern consciousness is given, is a datum, for contemporary thought. It is, if one prefers, an empirical a priori.

But now something else must be added immediately, to avoid a fatal misunderstanding: *To say that modern consciousness is an individual's situation is not to say that his experience and thought must irrevocably remain within the boundaries of this situation*. In other words, to understand the sociohistorical situatedness of human life and thought is not necessarily a deterministic understanding. If it were so, incidentally, social change would be probably impossible. *Homo sa-piens* is a situated being, but also a being forever driven to transcend his situation. Certainly, individuals differ in their capacity to transcend the situation into which the accident of birth has thrown them: There are a thousand dull conformists for every Socrates. Also, different sociohistorical situations entail different probabilities that an individual will transcend the boundaries of his situation: Athens was a more probable location for a Socrates than a starving village in the mountains of Thrace. Still, the principle remains that the situation in which the individual finds himself is the *starting point* of his life and thought; the *end point* of either is not inexorably predetermined, even if it may be predicted with a measure of probability.[3]

If one understands modern consciousness in this way, a number of important consequences follow. Most important of all, modern consciousness, even though it is recognized as the situation in which the contemporary thinker finds himself and with which he must reckon at least as his starting point, loses its quality of taken-for-granted superiority. Modern consciousness is one of many historically available forms of consciousness. It has specific characteristics, brought about and maintained by specific sociohistorical forces. It is changing and, like all human constructions in history, will eventually disappear or be transmuted into something quite different. Put simply, modern consciousness is a fact, but not necessarily one before which one must stand in awe. Of course modern man tends to think of himself and of his thoughts as the climax of evolution to date. In this he is no different from just about any preceding variety of the species. But there is no compelling reason why his claims should be given more weight than all the earlier ones. These claims themselves can be understood as the outcome of empirically given forces (such as the mind-boggling achievements of recent technology, which have something like a built-in megalomanic factor). The disciplines of history and of the social sciences can put modern consciousness in such a proper empirical perspective. This perspective, of course, does not yet provide a basis for deciding whether this or that claim of modern consciousness is finally valid or not. What it does provide is an attitude of soberness in which these claims can be assessed. Put differently, the empirical understanding of modern consciousness does not and cannot answer the philosophical questions as to the truth claims of modern man, but it is a highly useful prelude for this philosophical enterprise.

Thus, for example, it has been asserted that modern man is incapable of mythological thought—that is, of a perspective in which the universe is permeated by various divine or otherwise metahuman interventions. Let it be stipulated for the moment that this assertion is correct, at least in a statistical sense: The average middle-class American, upon having a vision of a demon, is more likely to call a psychiatrist than an exorcist. This probability is empirically available, and it can be explained in terms of the empirical determinants of this individual's situation. The intervention of demons in human life is a possibility excluded from the definitions of reality that have dominated this individual's socialization and education, and it is also excluded from the reality that is posited by the major institutions that surround him every day. In other words, there is no mystery about his probable reaction. Furthermore, the particular definitions of reality that govern his situation can be explained, in principle, by the history within which his own biography is but an episode; it could well be, for instance, that the role of technology in that history is one explanatory factor. So far, so good. The question remains: Are there demons? And, if so, did one sneak into Cleveland last night? The empirical finding that this individual, in his time and place, cannot conceive of the possibility is no answer to these questions. It is, after all, possible that the individual who cannot conceive of demons is making a big mistake. Extending this observation, it is possible that modern consciousness, while expanding man's awareness of some aspects of the universe, has made him lose sight of other aspects that are equally real.

Modern consciousness, for reasons that will be further elaborated in a moment, has a powerfully relativizing effect on all worldviews. To a large extent, the history of Western thought over the last few centuries has been one long effort to cope with the vertigo of relativity induced by modernization. Different analysts may opt for different proof texts for the start of all this. A pretty good one would be Pascal's statement that what is truth on one side of the Pyrenees is error on the other. As this insight became more widespread and more profound, the question as to who is right as between the two sides of the Pyrenees attained a particular urgency, which is one of the foremost characteristics of recent Western thought. An empirical understanding of the situation making for this cannot deliver anyone from the vertigo of relativity. It may even, for a while, increase the vertigo. Yet it also points to a way out—by relativizing the relativizing processes. Modernity is then perceived as a great relativizing caldron. But modernity itself is a relative phenomenon; it is one moment in the historical movements of human consciousness—not its pinnacle, or its culmination, or its end.

There have been two antithetical attitudes toward modernity from the beginning. The one has been an exaltation of modernity, celebrating it in terms of the idea of progress or some comparably optimistic view of history. The other has been to bemoan modernity as a vast degeneration, a fall from grace, even a dehumanizing event. The attitude suggested by the above considerations is different from either of these antitheses.

It is neither a celebration nor a lament over modernity; thus is neither "progressive" nor "reactionary." Modernity is a historical phenomenon like any other. As such, it is inevitably a mixture of admirable and deplorable features. And very likely it is also a mixture of truths and errors. It may be well to keep this attitude in mind throughout the following argument.

From Fate to Choice

Modern consciousness, like modernity in its external aspects, is an exceedingly complex aggregate of elements. Some of these are so closely connected with the institutions that form the core of modernity that it is difficult if not impossible to "think them away"—that is, to conceive of modern consciousness without these elements. For example, it is very hard to imagine a modern society without the sort of consciousness that makes telephonic communication feasible. Some other elements of modern consciousness are clearly not of this type. Rather, they are accidents of history that can be "thought away" without much trouble—such as, for example, the fact that the English language (and with it, of course, its freight of semantic and even poetic accouterments) has become the major vehicle of international communications in much of the world.[4] Now, one of the elements of modern consciousness that is very hard indeed to "think away" is the one already mentioned—the multiplication of options. Put differently, *modern consciousness entails a movement from fate to choice.*

Premodern man lived in what was, for the most part, a world of fate. This is so, of course, in the most obvious sense that a wide array of choices opened up by modern technology did not exist for him. Instead of a wide range of electrically powered tools, for instance, the premodern putterer-around-the-house

had but one single tool—say, the stone hammer handed down
ceremonially from father to son, either that very same hammer
or another shaped in exactly the same way. Instead of a wide
range of clothing styles, for another instance, the individual
had one single style, which was predetermined by the materials
and the tailoring techniques available as well as by tradition.
This last phrase, however, introduces another factor, which,
while related to the technological possibilities, already goes beyond the technological area proper. Thus an individual in a
premodern society would have been unlikely to vary his style in
clothing even if such an option were suddenly opened up to
him by this or that historical accident. This fact is precisely
what tradition is all about: One employs this tool, for a particular purpose, and no other. One dresses in this particular way,
and in no other. A traditional society is one in which the great
part of human activity is governed by such clear-cut pre-
scriptions. Whatever else may be the problems of a traditional
society, ambivalence is not one of them.

As modernity impinges on a traditional society, this world of
fate is shaken, often quickly and dramatically. This process can
still be observed in many places in the Third World today. No
more dramatic case exists than that of birth control. For all the
centuries of history prior to the advent of modern contraceptive techniques, sexuality and pregnancy were linked together in a relation of fate. To be sure, one could avoid pregnancy by avoiding sex, and there were various rudimentary
techniques to prevent conception. But none of these could
properly be called control. If not fate, then it was fortune that
ruled in this area of life. Modern contraception, for the first
time, has made pregnancy or nonpregnancy a matter of deliberate and reasonably reliable decision for millions of individuals.
In the most elementary way (and few things are as elemental

as those that affect one's own body) what before was fate has
now become a choice. The difficulties of birth-control cam-
paigns in many Third World countries, incidentally, can probably be explained to a considerable degree by the difficulty
traditional people have in grasping this truly Promethean
transformation. The birth-control advocate trying to propagate
this or that contraceptive technique in a traditional village is
not just peddling an interesting new gadget. Rather, he is
suggesting that the villagers rise in rebellion against what has
been destiny from times immemorial—and use their own bodies as instruments in this rebellion!

Sociologically speaking, premodern societies are marked by
the fact that their institutions have a very high degree of taken-
for-granted certainty. This is not to say that this certainty is
total; if it were, there would never have been any social change.
But the degree of certainty, when compared to that in a modern society, is very high indeed. What was said before about
the material techniques of life can also be said about the widest
range of institutional arrangements: This is how things are
done, and not in any other way. This is how one marries (and
whom); this is how one raises children, makes one's livelihood,
exercises power, goes to war—and in no other way. And, since
human beings derive their identity from what they do, this is
who one is—and one could not be anyone or anything else. In
any human society there is a connection between the network
of institutions and the, so to speak, available repertoire of identities. In a traditional society this connection is very much
closer than in a modern society. What is more, traditional institutions and identities are taken for granted, certain, almost
as objective as the facts of nature. In other words, both society
and self are experienced as fate.

In human experience, an objective fact is one about which

the individual has no choice, or, somewhat more precisely, which narrowly determines his choices. Gravity is an inexorable law of the objective world, and this fact cannot be ignored, "thought away," chosen to be nonexistent. To build a house beneath a hanging rock is to expose it to this objective facticity. If and when the rock begins to fall, the individual can try to run away, but the falling rock itself is an objective fact of the universe which, even if he curses it, he must accept. Premodern institutions and identities are objective in an analogous manner, in terms of how they are experienced. Their objectivity too is rocklike, and they "fall upon" the individual as fate or fortune decrees. To be born in this village is to live "under" these institutions, which "overhang" all of life from cradle to grave. And it means to live as a human being with highly profiled characteristics, which too are objectively given and recognized as such by others as well as by oneself.

This experience of objectivity is pretheoretical—that is, it precedes any systematic reflection about it. Quite simply, it is part and parcel of the fabric of ordinary, everyday living. But human beings do reflect, or at least some of them do. It is not surprising that in premodern societies the fate that is experienced in ordinary life also appears on the theoretical level. Put differently, *what is experienced as necessary is also interpreted as necessary*. These interpretations may take very different forms. In traditional societies most of them are rooted in mythology: The world is what it is because the gods have so decreed it. But the interpretations may also go beyond the mythological form and take on the quality of sophisticated speculation. The unfolding of the Greek notion of fate, *moira*, over several centuries of maturing thought is a fascinating instance of this.[5] Whatever their form, these interpretations ground the objective reality of social experience in an alleged objectivity of the cosmos. In this manner they provide an ultimate legitimation of the experienced necessities: What is must be, and it could be no other.[6]

The process by which modernity disrupts these worlds of fate is of key importance for the present argument and should therefore be elaborated in further detail. It is not possible to do this here with regard to the question whether technological proliferation per se has this effect, though enough has already been said to indicate that there is *some* connection between having different tools and different courses of action to choose from.[7] It is the proliferation of institutional choices that must be considered here. Modernity enormously complicates the institutional network of a society. The basic cause of this is the enormous complication of the division of labor, but the implications go far beyond the technological and economic areas of life first affected by this. *Modernity pluralizes.* Where there used to be one or two institutions, there now are fifty. Institutions, however, can best be understood as programs for human activity. Thus, what happens is that where there used to be one or two programs in a particular area of human life, there now are fifty. Not all of these new programs open up possibilities of individual choice. The fact that a contemporary citizen may now have to pay five different sets of taxes, while the subject of a traditional ruler only had to pay one tax, can hardly be looked upon as an opening up of options. But *some* of this institutional proliferation does have this consequence, and it is very important to understand that.

Take the area of sexual relations as a rather basic instance of this. A traditional society is almost invariably marked by a firm and quite narrow institutionalization of this area of human life: This is how things are done, and within this particular set of possible partners, and deviance from this pattern is severely sanctioned (assuming that deviance is conceivable and takes place at all). Modern societies in the West, and in America more than elsewhere, have seen a steady expansion of the range of accepted alternatives to the traditional pattern—in ever-widening tolerance of marriage beyond limited groups and in the definition of roles within the marriage relationship, as well as ever-widening tolerance of sexual relations before and outside marriage. The recent phenomena of the feminist and gay movements are thus an intensification of a considerably older trend of pluralization: A male individual now may not only marry a woman outside his racial, ethnic, religious, or class group, and he may not only enter into novel householding and child-rearing arrangements with his working wife, but he may choose to set up a permanent and open sexual relationship with another man. These recent movements, especially the last one, have introduced a sociologically very revealing term—that of "sexual life-style." Thus even sexuality can now be experienced as an arena of individual choices. All one has to do to grasp the dramatic change this entails is to try and explain to, say, an Indonesian—even a Western-educated intellectual—what Americans mean when they speak of "sexual life-styles"! The outcome of such an effort is likely to be not disapproval or revulsion but puzzlement if not sheer incomprehension. Nor is it at all clear that the pluralization of possible and socially acceptable courses of action in this area of life has reached an end. The recent developments in sex-change surgery suggest the possibility of even more radical choices: A woman may now choose not just a male role but a male body.[8] Again, the impact of this proliferation of possible programs for the individual can be summed up in the same formula: What previously was fate now becomes a set of choices. Or: Destiny is transformed into decision. And, again, this multiplication of choices is experienced on the pretheoretical level, by innumerable ordinary people with little or no interest in systematic reflection. Inevitably, though, this empirical situation calls out for interpretation—and *ipso facto* for systematic questioning of what used to be taken for granted as fate.

A Plurality of Worldviews

Thus the institutional pluralization that marks modernity affects not only human actions but also human consciousness: Modern man finds himself confronted not only by multiple options of possible courses of action but also by multiple options of possible ways of thinking about the world. In the fully modernized situation (of which contemporary America may be taken as the paradigm thus far) this means that the individual may choose his *Weltanschauung* very much as he chooses most other aspects of his private existence. In other words, there comes to be a smooth continuity between consumer choices in different areas of life—a preference for this brand of automobile as against another, for this sexual life-style as against another, and finally a decision to settle for a particular "religious preference." The truly mind-boggling implications of this last phrase, so common in ordinary American parlance, will be taken up shortly. For the moment, suffice it to say that there is a direct and sociologically analyzable link between the institutional and the cognitive transformations brought on by modernity.

This link can be put in more precise terms: *Modernity pluralizes both institutions and plausibility structures.* The last phrase represents a central concept for an understanding of the relationship between society and consciousness.[9] For the present purpose, its import can be stated quite simply. With the possible exception of a few areas of direct personal experience, human beings require social confirmation for their beliefs about reality. Thus the individual probably does not require others to convince him that he has a toothache, but he does require such social support for the whole range of his moral beliefs. Put differently, physical pain imposes its own plausibility without any social mediations, while morality requires particular social circumstances in order to become and remain plausible to the individual. It is precisely these social circumstances that constitute the plausibility structure for the morality at issue. For example, moral values of honor, courage, and loyalty are commonly characteristic of military institutions. As long as an individual is within such an institutional context, it is very likely that these values will be plausible to him in an unquestioned and taken-for-granted manner. If, however, this individual should find himself transposed into a quite different institutional context (say, there is no more need for many soldiers in his particular society, and he is forced by economic necessity to take up a civilian occupation), then it is very likely that he will begin to question the military values. Such a loss of plausibility is also the result of social processes—indeed, of the same kind of social processes that previously established and maintained the plausibility of the martial virtues. In the earlier situation other human beings provided social support for one set of moral values, as in the later situation social support is given to different moral values. Biographically, the individual may be seen as having migrated from one plausibility structure to another.

It follows from this that there is a direct relation between the cohesion of institutions and the subjective cohesiveness of beliefs, values, and worldviews. In a social situation in which everyone with whom the individual has significant ties is a soldier, it is not surprising that the soldier's view of the world, with all that this implies, will be massively plausible. Conversely, it is very difficult to be a soldier in a social situation where this makes little or no sense to everyone else. It may be added that this relation between social context and consciousness is not absolute. There are always exceptions—deviants or mavericks, individuals who maintain a view of the world and of themselves even in the absence of social support. These exceptions are always interesting, but they do not falsify the sociological generalization that human beliefs and values depend upon specific plausibility structures. In other words, this generalization is probabilistic—but the probability is very high indeed.

It further follows that the institutional pluralization of modernity had to carry in its wake a fragmentation and *ipso facto* a weakening of every conceivable belief and value dependent upon social support. The typical situation in which the individual finds himself in a traditional society is one where there are highly reliable plausibility structures. Conversely, modern societies are characterized by unstable, incohesive, unreliable plausibility structures. Put differently, in the modern situation certainty is hard to come by. It cannot be stressed enough that this fact is rooted in pretheoretical experience— that is, in ordinary, everyday social life. This experience is common to the proverbial man in the street and to the intellectual who spins out elaborate theories about the universe. The built-in uncertainty is common to both as well. This basic sociological insight is crucial for an understanding of the competition between worldviews and the resultant crisis of belief that has been characteristic of modernity.

The modern individual, then, lives in a world of choice, in sharp contrast with the world of fate inhabited by traditional man. He must choose in innumerable situations of everyday life, but this necessity of choosing reaches into the areas of beliefs, values, and worldviews. To decide, however, means to reflect. The modern individual must stop and pause where premodern men could act in unreflective spontaneity. Quite simply, the modern individual must engage in more deliberate thinking—*not* because he is more intelligent, *not* because he is on some sort of higher level of consciousness, *but* because his social situation forces him to this. He encounters the necessity to choose, and *ipso facto* the necessity of pausing to reflect before choosing, on various levels of life. Ordinary, everyday life is full of choices, from the most trivial choices between competing consumer commodities to far-reaching alternatives in lifestyle. Biography too is a sequence of choices, many if not most of them new to modernity—choices of educational and occupational careers, of marriage partners and "styles" of marriage, of alternative patterns of child-rearing, of a near-infinite variety of voluntary associations, of social and political commitments. These latter typically involve the individual in societal choices, some of them of vast scope—choices between alternative political programs for society as a whole, choices between "alternative futures" of every kind. In a historically unprecedented manner the modern individual plans his own life and that of his family, as modern societies plan their collective future. And, to repeat, this necessity to choose bridges the pretheoretical and theoretical levels of experience.

A further consequence of this situation, and a most curious one, has been a new measure of complexity in the individual's experience of himself: Modernization has brought with it a strong accentuation of the subjective side of human existence; indeed, it may be said that modernization and subjectivization are cognate processes.[10] This has often been remarked upon as far as theoretical thought, especially philosophy, is concerned. Thus, Western philosophy since Descartes has been characterized as a turning toward subjectivity. Epistemology, of course, expresses this by asking over and over again the question "What can I know?" It is very important to understand that this question not only is asked by philosophers but, under certain circumstances, becomes an urgent concern for the ordinary man in the street. Modernity produces such circumstances. But even under more reliable conditions human beings must have available some sort of answer to this question, if only because every new generation of children asks it in one way or another—and the adults must be in a position to reply. In a society with stable, coherent plausibility structures the answers can be given in a tone of great assurance. That is, the socially defined reality has a very high degree of objectivity: "This is what the world is like; it is this and no other; it could not be any different; so stop asking silly questions." It is precisely this type of objectivity that comes to be eroded by the forces of modernization. In consequence, the answers to the perennial human question "What can I know?" become uncertain, hesitating, anxious. Yet the individual must have some answers, because he must have some sort of meaningful order to live in and live by. If answers are not provided objectively by his society, he is compelled to turn *inward*, toward his own subjectivity, to dredge up from there whatever certainties he can manage. This inward turning is subjectivization, a process that embraces both Descartes and the man-in-the-street who is puzzled about the proper course of action in this or that area of everyday life.

If this point is understood, it should not be surprising that modern Western culture has been marked by an ever-increasing attention to subjectivity. Philosophy is only one small part of this. There is modern literature (the novel is the prime example here), modern art, and, last but not least, the astronomic proliferation of modern psychologies and psychotherapies. All of these, however, are manifestations of subjectivization on the level of theoretical thought. All of them are rooted in pretheoretical experience—fundamentally, in the experience that the socially defined universe can no longer be relied upon. Indeed, speaking of modern philosophy, one can put this by saying that the aforementioned social situation is its necessary plausibility structure. The same can be said of modern literature, art, and psychology (and, not so incidentally, of modern sociology). And all of this is very much connected with the transition from fate to choice: The taken-for-granted manner in which premodern institutions ordered human life is eroded. What previously was self-evident fact now becomes an occasion to choose. Fate does not require reflection; the individual who is compelled to make choices is also compelled to stop and think. The more choices, the more reflection. The individual who reflects inevitably becomes more conscious of himself. That is, he turns his attention from the objectively given outside world to his own subjectivity. As he does this, two things happen simultaneously: The outside world becomes more questionable, and his own inner world becomes more complex. Both of these things are unmistakable features of modern man.

A Very Nervous Prometheus

This modern man, as he undergoes the world-shattering movement from fate to choice, easily impresses one as a Promethean figure. Often enough, especially since the Enlightenment, he has so impressed himself. It is all the more important to see that he is a very nervous Prometheus. For the transition from fate to choice is experienced in a highly ambivalent manner. On the one hand, it is a great liberation; on the other hand, it is anxiety, alienation, even terror. One naturally thinks here first of some of the great thinkers of modernity—

Kierkegaard, or Nietzsche, or Dostoyevsky. But the ambivalence of liberation and alienation is experienced by countless human beings who have never read a book (let alone written one). Every Third World city today is full of such people. On the one hand, modernity attracts them like a powerful magnet, with its promises of new freedom, new possibilities of life and of self-realization. Needless to say, these promises are not always fulfilled, but modernity is in fact experienced as liberation —from the narrow confines of tradition, of poverty, of the bonds of clan and tribe. On the other hand, a very high price is exacted for this liberation. The individual comes to experience himself as being *alone* in a way that is unthinkable in traditional society—deprived of the firm solidarity of his collectivity, uncertain of the norms by which his life is to be governed, finally uncertain of who or what he is. An African villager cast adrift in the tumultuous world of, say, Lagos or Nairobi will hardly have heard of modern European philosophy. Yet he will be able to testify, in the living reality of his existence if not in words, what it means to be "condemned to freedom." Philosophers may argue whether this phrase of Sartre's is an adequate formulation of the human condition; the sociologist must say that it admirably sums up the condition of *modern* man; the sociologist can add that only under modern social circumstances could such a philosophical proposition have attained widespread plausibility.

Liberation and alienation are inextricably connected, reverse sides of the same coin of modernity.[11] To want the first without the second is one of the recurring fantasies of the modern revolutionary imagination; to perceive the second without the first is the Achilles' heel of virtually all conservative viewpoints. Yet one must beware lest one exaggerate the alienated desperation of most modern individuals. It is simply not true that most people live in a state of prolonged *Angst;* Camus was right against Sartre on this point, and in retrospect one suspects that in the same way Bishop Mynster was right against Kierkegaard, as Jacob Burckhardt was against Nietzsche. Most people manage somehow. Some continue to live in and by the remnants of traditional structures; others have succeeded in constructing various new arrangements that afford a measure of certainty; others again just keep themselves very busy. The point then is definitely *not* that modern men are all do-it-yourself existentialists, tottering on the brink of an abyss of despair. Rather, the point is that the business of "arranging oneself in the universe" (the phrase, freely translated, is by Ernst Bloch) has become considerably more difficult than in a traditional society. For some, of course, it has become impossibly difficult, but their case should not be generalized. All the same, even this more moderated, non-Kierkegaardian description of the modern condition should make clear that the latter is something of a *novum* in history. Nor is it necessary, in order to grasp the implications of this, to assert that the modern situation is *totally* unprecedented. There are some parallels to other periods when previously taken-for-granted orders were shaken, as for example in the Hellenistic period. It is likely, however, that never before was the pluralization of meanings and values experienced as massively by as many people. The reason for this, of course, must be sought in modern technology: The sense of relativity too can be mass-communicated.

The alienating aspect of modernity has, from the beginning, brought forth nostalgias for a restored world of order, meaning, and solidarity. One way of stating this is that modernization and countermodernization are always cognate processes.[12] The yearning for deliverance from the alienations of modernity may take quite different forms. Its more straightforward form is the one commonly called "reactionary." This is expressed theoretically in ideologies that look to the past for meaning while they perceive the present as a state of degeneration; the expression of these ideologies in sociopolitical praxis is in attempts (typically Quixotic) to restore structures that preceded modernity. But there is also a so-called "progressive" form of this redemptive yearning. Here the present is also perceived as dehumanized and intolerable, but the restored world is not sought in the past but rather is projected into the future. This form of countermodernity is typical of modern revolutionary ideologies and movements. Marxism is the prototypical case, and its great attractiveness cannot be understood apart from its affinity for countermodern nostalgias.

Is the movement from fate to choice irreversible? In principle, nothing historical is irreversible. But it is very difficult to see how, given the necessary technological foundations of sustaining life for numbers such as now inhabit the earth, this movement could be reversed very easily. There is a built-in plurality and *ipso facto* a built-in instability to the institutional arrangements necessitated by this situation. There is, however, one very important exception to this statement: the modern totalitarian state. Its central goal is the restoration of a premodern order of stable meanings and firm collective solidarity. The paradox is that, in seeking this goal, it employs the most modern means of communication and control—means that are, in and of themselves, alienating in their effect. Modern totalitarianism is a very recent phenomenon; even if defined most broadly, it is only some fifty years old. It is too early to say whether the experiment has failed. It is not too early to say that its empirical success would be a human tragedy of unprecedented scope. Of all possible "solutions" to the discontents of modernity this one, surely, is not one in which to invest hope for humanity. It follows that, in rejecting the totalitarian possibility of a new world of fate, one will have to find ways of coping with the world of choice.

The Heretical Imperative

It will be clear by now that religion is by no means the only area of experience and thought affected by the transition from fate to choice. Morality, for one, is crucially affected, as are all institutions (notably political ones) that lay claim to any kind of moral authority. But the modern situation of religion will remain inadequately explained unless its relation to the aforementioned transition is understood.

The impact of modernity on religion is commonly seen in terms of the process of secularization, which can be described simply as one in which religion loses it hold on the level both of institutions and of human consciousness. This is not the place to review the by-now immense literature on the causes, character, and historical course of secularization.[13] But one point should be made here: At the very least, there is a close connection between secularization and the pluralization of plausibility structures described above. Nor are the reasons for this hard to understand. A religious worldview, just like any other body of interpretations of reality, is dependent upon social support. The more unified and reliable this support is, the more these interpretations of reality will be firmly established in consciousness. The typical premodern society creates conditions under which religion has, for the individual, the quality of objective certainty; modern society, by contrast, undermines this certainty, deobjectivates it by robbing it of its taken-for-granted status, *ipso facto* subjectivizes religion. And this change, of course, is directly related to the transition from fate to choice: The premodern individual was linked to his gods in the same inexorable destiny that dominated most of the rest of his existence; modern man is faced with the necessity of choosing between gods, a plurality of which are socially available to him. If the typical condition of premodern man is one of religious certainty, it follows that that of modern man is one of religious doubt. Needless to say, this difference is not absolute. There were premodern individuals who struggled with religious doubt, as there are people today with unshaken religious convictions. The difference is one of, so to speak, frequency distributions. The frequency of religious uncertainty in the modern situation, however, is so drastically greater that it is valid to embody it within a notion of typicality. Whatever other causes there may be for modern secularization, it should be clear that the pluralizing process has had secularizing effects in and of itself.

The English word "heresy" comes from the Greek verb *hairein*, which means "to choose." A *hairesis* originally meant, quite simply, the taking of a choice. A derived meaning is that of an opinion. In the New Testament, as in the Pauline epistles, the word already has a specifically religious connotation—that of a faction or party within the wider religious community; the rallying principle of such a faction or party is the particular religious opinion that its members have chosen. Thus, in Galatians 5:20 the apostle Paul lists "party spirit" (*hairesis*) along with such evils as strife, selfishness, envy, and drunkenness among the "works of the flesh." In the later development of Christian ecclesiastical institutions, of course, the term acquired much more specific theological and legal meanings. Its etymology remains sharply illuminating.

For this notion of heresy to have any meaning at all, there was presupposed the authority of a religious tradition. Only with regard to such an authority could one take a heretical attitude. The heretic denied this authority, refused to accept the tradition *in toto*. Instead, he picked and chose from the contents of the tradition, and from these pickings and choosings constructed his own deviant opinion. One may suppose that this possibility of heresy has always existed in human communities, as one may suppose that there have always been rebels and innovators. And, surely, those who represented the authority of a tradition must always have been troubled by the possibility. Yet the social context of this phenomenon has changed radically with the coming of modernity: *In premodern situations there is a world of religious certainty, occasionally ruptured by heretical deviations. By contrast, the modern situation is a world of religious uncertainty, occasionally staved off by more or less precarious constructions of religious affirmation.* Indeed, one could put this change even more sharply: *For premodern man, heresy is a possibility—usually a rather remote one; for modern man, heresy typically becomes a necessity.* Or again, *modernity creates a new situation in which picking and choosing becomes an imperative.*

Now, suddenly, heresy no longer stands out against a clear background of authoritative tradition. The background has become dim or even disappeared. As long as that background was still there, individuals had the possibility of *not* picking and choosing—they could simply surrender to the taken-for-granted consensus that surrounded them on all sides, and that is what most individuals did. But now this possibility itself becomes dim or disappears: How can one surrender to a consensus that is socially unavailable? Any affirmation must first create the consensus, even if this can only be done in some small quasi-sectarian community. In other words, individuals now *must* pick and choose. Having done so, it is very difficult to forget the fact. There remains the memory of the deliberate construction of a community of consent, and with this a haunting sense of the *constructedness* of that which the community affirms. Inevitably, the affirmations will be fragile and this fragility will not be very far from consciousness.

An example may serve here; it is perhaps the most important example in the modern Western world—that of Jewish emancipation. In the situation of the ghetto, as in the *shtetl* of eastern Europe, it would have been absurd to say that an individual *chose* to be a Jew. To be Jewish was a taken-for-granted given of the individual's existence, ongoingly reaffirmed with ringing certainty by everyone in the individual's milieu (including the non-Jews in that milieu). There was the theoretical possibility of conversion to Christianity, but the social pressures against this were so strong that it was realized in very few cases. There were, to be sure, different versions of being Jewish, and even the possibility of being a rather poor specimen of a Jew, but none of these really touched the massive objective and subjective reality of being a Jew. The coming of emancipation changed all this. For more and more individuals it became a viable project to step outside the Jewish community. Suddenly, to be Jewish emerged as one choice among others. Ethnicity internally and anti-Semitism externally served to brake this development, but it went quite far in central and western Europe in the nineteenth century. The fullest development was reached in America in the twentieth century. Today, within the pluralistic dynamic of American society, there must be very few individuals indeed for whom being Jewish has the quality of a taken-for-granted fact.

Yet those who affirm an orthodox or even a moderately orthodox version of Jewish identity continue to define the latter as such a fact. Their problem is that they must affirm it in the face of empirical evidence to the contrary. The orthodox precisely defines Jewish identity as destiny, while the social experience of the individual reveals it as an ongoing choice. This dis-

sonance between definition and experience is at the core of
every orthodoxy in the modern world (the Jewish case is just a
particularly clear case of a much more general phenomenon):
The orthodox defines himself as living in a tradition; it is of the
very nature of tradition to be taken for granted; this taken-for-
grantedness, however, is continually falsified by the experience
of living in a modern society. The orthodox must then present
to himself as fate what he knows empirically to be a choice.
This is a difficult feat. It goes far to explain the attraction of
such movements as that of Lubavitcher Hassidism, which con-
structs an artificial *shtetl* for its followers. The difference from
the old *shtetl* is, quite simply, this: All the individual has to do
to get out of his alleged Jewish destiny is to walk out and take
the subway. Outside, waiting, is the emporium of life-styles,
identities, and religious preferences that constitutes American
pluralism. It is hard to believe that this empirical fact can be
altogether pushed out of consciousness by an individual reared
in America, even if his conversion to a neotraditional existence has been intensely fervent. That existence, consequently,
has a fragility that is totally alien to a genuinely traditional
community.

The weight of the peculiarly American phrase "religious preference" may now have become apparent. It contains within itself the whole crisis into which pluralism has plunged religion.
It points to a built-in condition of cognitive dissonance—and
to the heretical imperative as a root phenomenon of modernity.

To sum up the argument thus far: Modernity multiplies
choices and concomitantly reduces the scope of what is experienced as destiny. In the matter of religion, as indeed in other
areas of human life and thought, this means that the modern
individual is faced not just with the opportunity but with the
necessity to make choices as to his beliefs. This fact constitutes
the heretical imperative in the contemporary situation. Thus

2

Religion:
Experience, Tradition,
Reflection

WHEN THE EXTERNAL (that is, socially available) authority of tradition declines, individuals are forced to become more reflective, to ask themselves the question of what they really know and what they only imagined themselves to know in the old days when the tradition was still strong. Such reflection, just about inevitably, will further compel individuals to turn to their own experience: Man is an empirical animal (if one prefers, an *anima naturaliter scientifica*) to the extent that his own direct experience is always the most convincing evidence of the reality of anything. The individual, say, believes in X. As long as all people around him, including the "reality experts" of his society, ongoingly affirm the same X, his belief is carried easily, spontaneously, by this social consensus. This is no longer possible when the consensus begins to disintegrate, when competing "reality experts" appear on the scene. Sooner or later, then, the individual will have to ask himself, "But do I *really* believe in X? Or could it be that X has been an illusion all heresy, once the occupation of marginal and eccentric types, has become a much more general condition; indeed, heresy has become universalized.

The rest of this book will discuss the implications of this situation, in terms both of understanding it and of using it as a point of departure for constructive religious reflection. It should be clear from the beginning that confronting the heretical imperative has not been easy for the religious mind—not for the mind of the simple believer, nor for that of the most sophisticated theologian. On all levels of sophistication one may observe a spectrum of reactions, ranging from a total rejection of the new situation to a total embrace of it. Later chapters will spell out the difficulties of both rejection and embrace. It may be an oversimplification to say that the history of Christian theology in the modern West has been the drama of this confrontation with the heretical imperative, but it is probably not too much of an oversimplification. Judaism in the modern West has undergone the same confrontation in a somewhat different form, due, of course, to the distinctive relation of religion to the social position of the Jews in a predominantly Christian culture. Today, as modernization has become a worldwide phenomenon no longer restricted to its Western matrix, the confrontation with the heretical imperative has also become worldwide. It can be observed in the most sophisticated discussions at, say, Buddhist centers of learning or a centuries-old Muslim universities—but also in the homespun advice being given to illiterate villagers by religious functionaries barely able to read their holy scriptures. If nothing else, this has given all the religions in the world a commonality of condition that must have an effect on their self-understanding—and should have an effect on their relations with each other. That point will also be taken up again later.

along?" And then will come the other question: "Just what has been *my own experience* of X?"

This cognitive dynamics pertains, in principle, to any belief —or, more precisely, to any belief that goes beyond the immediate self-authentication of a toothache. In the preceding chapter the argument was made that it pertains with particular sharpness to the area of religious beliefs, and that modernity has produced a built-in crisis for religion in consequence of this dynamics. It follows that the modern situation, with its weakened hold of religious tradition over the consciousness of individuals, must lead to much more deliberate reflection about the character and the evidential status of religious experience. This is, in fact, what has happened—first in the Western cultural matrix of modernity (and with special virulence in Protestantism, which, of all religious complexes, has had the most intimate relation to modernity), and then throughout the world in the wake of the modernization process. To say, then, that the weakening of tradition *must* lead to a new attention to experience is not just a theoretical proposition. Rather, it serves to explain what has actually taken place.

It seems obvious, though, that the term "experience" requires clarification at this point in the argument: *Whose* experience is at issue here? And *what* is supposedly experienced? Such clarification is the purpose of this chapter.

Now an important distinction must be made immediately— that between the individuals whom Max Weber so aptly called the "religious virtuosi" and everyone else. There are individuals, mystics and the like, who claim to have had direct personal experience of religious realities. One may say that, for such individuals, religious beliefs *are* as immediately self-authenticating as the experience of a toothache. They may indeed reflect about their own experience, and some of the great mystics have also been great thinkers. What they will reflect about, though, is unlikely to be the *reality* of their religious experiences but rather the *relation* of these experiences to all sorts of other things (including the tradition they find in their social milieu). The rest of humanity is in a more complicated situation. Those who are not "religious virtuosi" have had, at best, fugitive and intimational experiences in this area, and most of their religious beliefs are grounded in a socially mediated tradition. Yet they also have a certain advantage: Not having had the kind of experience that leads to an undeniable conviction of reality, they can with some detachment look for evidence in the accounts of those who claim to have had such experience. In other words, they have the advantage of the dentist over his patient in any effort to undertake a comprehensive investigation of the phenomenon "toothache."

Let it be assumed, then, that the present argument proceeds within such a situation. That is, neither author nor reader is assumed to have had the kind of experiences that produce a never-to-be-denied-again sense of reality. (One may add, incidentally, that if either author or reader, let alone both, could claim such experiences, the argument would be either impossible or unnecessary!) The reflective process of an individual in this situation can be formulated as follows: "I have not seen the gods; they have not spoken to me; neither have I experienced the divine within myself. I must begin my thinking about religion with the acknowledgment that this fact precludes any affirmations that are unquestionable, undeniably real, or absolutely certain. I have indeed had intimations, intuitions, of the gods in my own experience, and I will reflect about these to see what evidential value they may have. I have also been shaped in my thinking about religion by the tradition or traditions that have dominated my social milieu; what is more, there are specific experiences that have been mediated by this tradition or these traditions. Thus, for example, some of my intimations of the gods have taken place in the course of my participation in rituals of my own tradition or even of other traditions that I have encountered during my life. As I reflect about religion, I will take the traditional affirmations and any experiences linked to them as possible evidence. Furthermore, I have available to me accounts and reports of those who have claimed to have seen the gods, to have been addressed by them, or to have had direct experience of the divine. These accounts and reports also constitute possible evidence. In acknowledging my situation of uncertainty, I find myself compelled to be both skeptical and selective in dealing with the evidence. If I retain this attitude, I must be open to the possibility that my quest will end in the same uncertainty in which it began as well as to the possibility that, perhaps surprisingly, it will end in certainty."

Such an attitude, of course, is by no means unique to the present moment in history; the reasons why it is singularly appropriate to this moment have already been given. But another point should be stressed: What is just about unique in the modern situation is the *sheer availability* of the aforementioned accounts and reports of the multiform religious experience of mankind. Certainly this is the case in America. An individual willing to spend, say, some two hundred dollars can walk into any better bookstore in this country and purchase a collection of paperback books containing good translations, with commentary, of most of the key writings of the world's great religions. If the individual is in a metropolitan area or near a large university, it is likely that, in addition to reading the books he has purchased, he will find groups that actually adhere to these religious beliefs or academic courses that deal with them more or less competently. Such a situation has never existed in history before. It provides a great opportunity for following up the above-described attitude toward the evidence of other people's religious experiences and traditions. It is also, of course, part and parcel of what has previously been designated the heretical imperative of the contemporary situation: An individual can, of course, refrain from buying all these paperbacks and avoid contact with the variegated religious expressions available in his social environment—but that too would be a choice on his part.

The concern of this book is to explore the possibilities of passing from this situation to positive religious affirmations, to statements about the world that can plausibly be prefaced by the words "I believe." This project proposes that the heretical imperative can be turned from an obstacle to an aid both to religious faith and to reflection about it. The project, of course, is in itself an act of reflection: This book is an argument, an exercise in religious thought, *not* a confessional document or a guide to religious experience. It is all the more important to keep in mind that religion is not primarily a matter of reflection or of theorizing. At the heart of the religious phenomenon is prereflective, pretheoretical experience. What must be done now is to look more closely at the character of this experience.

Many Realities

If the religious phenomenon is approached in the empirical attitude just described, it is clear that it will, at the very least initially, appear as a *human* phenomenon. That is, if the intention is to locate what is commonly called religious experience within a wider spectrum of human experiences, then, at least while this inquiry is being undertaken, all metahuman explanations of the phenomenon must be bracketed, put aside. Such an inquiry by no means implies that metahuman explanations are ruled out a priori, or that the individual undertaking the inquiry confesses himself an atheist, but only that for the moment he respects the limits of this kind of inquiry. All of this can be summed up by saying that the method employed here belongs to the phenomenology of religion; for the present purpose, the term "phenomenology" may be understood quite simply as a method that investigates a phenomenon in terms of the manner in which it appears in human experience, without immediately raising the question of its ultimate status in reality.[1]

Reality is not experienced as one unified whole. Rather, human beings experience reality as containing zones or strata with greatly differing qualities. This fundamental fact is what Alfred Schutz called the experience of multiple realities.[2] For instance, the individual experiences one zone of reality when dreaming, a quite different zone while awake. For another instance, there is a zone of reality one enters in intense aesthetic experience (say, "getting lost" in listening to a piece of music), and this zone is quite different from the reality of ordinary, everyday activities. Now, there is one reality that has a privileged character in consciousness, and it is precisely the reality of being wide awake in ordinary, everyday life. That is, this reality is experienced as *more real*, and as more real *most of the time*, as compared with other experienced realities (such as those of dreams or of losing oneself in music). For this reason Schutz called it the paramount reality. The other realities, as seen from its standpoint, appear as some sort of enclaves into which consciousness moves and from which it returns to the "real world" of everyday life. Schutz accordingly called these other realities finite provinces of meaning; he also used a term coined by William James, that of subuniverses.

The paramount reality, then, is reality as it is experienced when one is wide awake and engaged in the activities that one normally identifies with ordinary, everyday life. Now, this is also the reality one shares most easily with other people. The individual coinhabits it with large numbers of other human beings, who ongoingly confirm its existence and its major characteristics. Indeed, it is this ongoing social confirmation that goes far in explaining its paramount status in consciousness; repeating a phrase used in the preceding chapter, it is this reality that has the strongest plausibility structure (as against, say, the reality of dreams or musical experience).

These are not abstruse theoretical considerations but rather are explications of very common experiences. Suppose one falls asleep—perhaps while working at one's desk—and has a vivid dream. The reality of the dream begins to pale as soon as one returns to a wakeful state, and one is then conscious of having temporarily left the mundane reality of everyday life. That mundane reality remains the point of departure and orientation, and when one comes back to it, this return is commonly described as "coming back to reality"—that is, precisely, coming back to the paramount reality. Thus, from the standpoint of the paramount reality, other realities are experienced as alien zones, enclaves, or "holes" within it. To say this, again, is not making a theoretical statement about the ultimate constitution of being. Perhaps, who knows, this mundane reality may ultimately turn out to be an illusion. In the meantime, however, it is experienced in this particular way, most of the time and (to use another Jamesian term) with the strongest accent of reality.

The central paradox of the paramount reality is that it is *both* massively real (*realissimum*) *and* very precarious. The former characteristic is due to the massive character of the supporting social confirmation (virtually everyone one encounters shares it), the latter to the fact that these supporting social processes are inherently fragile and easily interrupted—as, indeed, by the simple accident of falling asleep. Schutz puts this rather nicely by saying that the accent of reality of ordinary, everyday life pertains "until further notice." Put differently, the paramount reality is easily ruptured. As soon as that happens, it is immediately relativized and the individual then finds himself in a quite different world (which, by the way, is exactly how he is likely to describe the occurrence).

Most of the time, then, the individual is conscious of being situated in the massively real world of ordinary, everyday life, along with most other human beings of his acquaintance (the few lunatics or other eccentrics he may know are unlikely to disturb this consciousness). But the individual also experiences ruptures in this mundane reality; these ruptures are experienced as limits or boundaries of the paramount reality. They are of quite different sorts: Some are clearly based on physiological processes—such as dreams, the borderline states between sleep and wakefulness, intense physical sensations (painful or pleasurable), hallucinatory experiences (such as those caused by drugs). The paramount reality, however, may also be ruptured in experiences that seem to lack any physiological basis—such as the experiences of theoretical abstraction (as when the world "dissolves" in the abstractions of theoretical physics or pure mathematics), aesthetic experience, or the experience of the comic. As he undergoes such an experience of rupture, the individual suddenly finds himself as standing outside the mundane world, which now appears to him as flawed, absurd, or even illusionary. Its accent of reality suddenly diminishes or vanishes. Thus all these rupturing experiences are ecstatic in character, in the literal sense of ekstasis, of "standing outside" the ordinary world. This ecstatic quality belongs to a dream as it does to the subuniverse of a joke, to all experiences of "being lost to the world"—be it in an orgasm, or in Mozart's music, or in the intoxicating abstractions of quantum theory.

From within the experience of any one of these ecstatic ruptures, the ordinary world not only is relativized but is now seen to have a previously unperceived quality. This could be described by the German term *Doppelbödigkeit*; the term derives from the theater and literally means "having a double floor." The ordinary world, previously perceived as massive and cohesive, is now seen as being tenuously put together, like a stage-set made of cardboard, full of holes, easily collapsed into unreality. Furthermore, behind the newly revealed holes in the fabric of this world appears *another reality*. One now understands that this other reality has been there all along—on "another floor," as it were. In other words, the experience of *Doppelbödigkeit* not only reveals an unfamiliar new reality but throws a new light on the familiar reality of ordinary experience.[3]

One can have this experience in very different degrees. There are mild shocks to the reality of the ordinary world that can be dismissed rather easily: "This was just a bad dream"; or, "I only feel this way because of my damn toothache"; or, "Oh, I see, you were only joking." But there are also severe jolts to the paramount reality, with consequences in consciousness that remain even after one has returned to the world of ordinary, everyday life: "I will never be able to forget what the world was like when I took LSD"; or, "Since my mid-thirties I have developed a sense of humor that makes me see life in a very different way"; or, "Life has never been the same for me since the death of my mother." Moreover, there are different avenues by which an individual arrives at experiences of reality—rupture. Some individuals try to get there through deliberate efforts—by taking drugs, for example, or by cultivating certain types of aesthetic experience, or even by embarking on a physical adventure (climbing Mount Everest, say) with the express purpose of changing one's sense of life. Other experiences of reality-rupture are involuntary. Experiences of illness or death are rarely sought after, but the development of a sense of humor in mid-life may take one by surprise too. What all these experiences have in common is that they open up realities that are, literally, "beyond this world"—beyond, that is, the world of ordinary, everyday existence. In principle, every such "other reality" can be described, although any attempt at description suffers from the fact that language has its roots in mundane experience. This is why all "other realities," from a toothache to Mozart's music, are "difficult to talk about" (and, of course, virtually impossible to talk about with someone who has not had a similar experience).

Religion as Experience

None of the aforementioned experiences of reality-rupture would commonly be called religious. The omission has been deliberate, for the purpose of the present argument is to *locate* those experiences commonly called religious within a broader spectrum of human experiences. Empirically speaking, what is commonly called religion involves an aggregate of human attitudes, beliefs, and actions in the face of two types of experience —the experience of the supernatural and the experience of the sacred. The character of these two experiences must now be clarified.

The experience of the supernatural is one specific "other reality" of the kind just described.[4] From the standpoint of ordinary reality, of course, it too has the quality of a finite province of meaning from which one "returns to reality"—returns, that is, to the world of ordinary, everyday life. A crucial aspect of the supernatural, as against other finite provinces of meaning, is its radical quality. The reality of this experience, the world of the supernatural, is radically, overwhelmingly *other*. What is encountered is a complete world set over against the world of mundane experience. What is more, when seen in the perspective of this other world, the world of ordinary experience is now seen as a sort of *antechamber*. The status of enclave, or finite province of meaning, is thus radically transposed: The supernatural is now no longer an enclave within the ordinary world; rather, the supernatural looms over, "haunts," even envelopes the ordinary world. There now emerges the conviction that the other reality opened up by the experience is the true *realissimum*, is ultimate reality, by comparison with which ordinary reality pales into insignificance.

It must be strongly emphasized that the experience of the supernatural opens up the vista of a cohesive and comprehensive world. This other world is perceived as having been there all along, though it was not previously perceived, and it forces itself upon consciousness as an undeniable reality, as a force bidding one to enter it. The world of the supernatural is perceived as being "out there," as having an irresistible reality that is independent of one's own will, and it is this massively objective character that contests the old reality status of the ordinary world.

The radical quality of the experience of the supernatural is further manifested by its inner organization. There is the sense of startling and totally certain insights. The image of a sudden passage from darkness to light recurs in the accounts of the experience. Within the experience the categories of ordinary existence are transformed, especially the categories of space and time. Recurringly the supernatural is conceived of as being located in a different dimension of space or of time. In terms of spatial symbols, it may be located "up above," as against the "here below" of earthly existence.[5] In terms of temporal symbols, it may be located in a different time, as biblical language distinguishes between "this aeon" and "the aeon that is to come."[6] There may well be important consequences to the choice between spatial and temporal symbols in this context (as biblical scholars have often insisted). But for the present purpose that choice is not decisive. *Either* form of symbolic expression points to the same underlying experience—one in which the categories of ordinary reality are radically contested, exploded, *aufgehoben*.

The experience of the supernatural also transforms the perception of both self and others. Within the experience one encounters oneself in a radically new and putatively ultimate manner, in a disclosure of one's "true self." This inevitably implies a different perception of other human beings and one's relationship to them. Very often this involves a sense of intense connection or love. Finally, the experience often (not always) entails encounters with other beings that are not accessible in ordinary reality. These may be the "true selves" of other human beings or of animals, or the "souls" of the dead, or supernatural beings with no embodiments in the ordinary world. In other words, the other world disclosed in the experience of the supernatural is often an *inhabited* world, and the encounter with these "inhabitants" will in these instances be an important aspect of the experience.

It will be clear from the foregoing that the history of religion must serve as the principal source for a description of the experience of the supernatural. It is all the more important to stress that this experience is *not* coextensive with the phenomenon of religion, or for that matter with what is commonly called mysticism. A brief word on definitions is necessary here. Religion, for the present purpose, may be defined as a human attitude that conceives of the cosmos (including the supernatural) as a sacred order.[7] The components of this definition could, of course, be elaborated upon at great length, but this is not the place to do so. What should be stressed here, though, is that the category of the sacred is central to this definition—to the

point, indeed, that religion could also be defined more simply
as a human attitude in the face of the sacred. This latter category, however, is not necessarily linked to the supernatural.
Thus human beings have taken on attitudes that can properly
be described as religious (as in rituals, emotional responses, and
cognitive beliefs) toward definitely mundane entities conceived
by them to be sacred—such as various social entities, from the
clan to the nation-state. Conversely, it is possible for human
beings to confront supernatural experiences in a definitely
nonreligious attitude, in a profane rather than sacred mode—
such as has always been the case with magicians and is the case
today with researchers in parapsychology. The supernatural and
the sacred are kindred phenomena, and historically it may be
assumed that the latter experience is rooted in the former. But
it is very important to keep the two apart analytically. One way
of conceiving their relationship is to think of the supernatural
and the sacred as two overlapping, but not coinciding, circles of
human experience.

Mysticism is, again, an important source for accounts of the
experience of the supernatural—but it is not the only one. Mysticism may be defined as an avenue to the supernatural by
means of immersion in the putative "depths" of an individual's
own consciousness.[8] Put differently, the mystic encounters the
supernatural within himself, as a reality that coincides with the
innermost recesses of his own self. There are, however, experiences of the supernatural that are quite different—to wit, experiences within which the supernatural is encountered as external to and possibly even antagonistic to the self or the
consciousness of the individual. A good case can be made that
mysticism has always been a marginal phenomenon in the
religious traditions derived from the Bible. Although there
have been eruptions of mysticism in these traditions, Judaism,
Christianity, and Islam are *au fond* nonmystical religions, in

which the sacred is encountered by the individual outside rather than within himself.[9] Conversely, there are forms of mysticism that do not involve a religious attitude at all.[10] Mysticism too, then, may be perceived as a phenomenon that intersects with, but is not to be equated with, the experience of the sacred.

The classical description of the experience of the sacred is the one by Rudolf Otto, and there is no need to elaborate on it here.[11] But two central and somewhat paradoxical characteristics should be emphasized here: The sacred is experienced as being utterly other (*totaliter aliter*); at the same time, it is experienced as being of immense and indeed redemptive significance for human beings. Both the metahuman otherness and the human significance of the sacred are intrinsic to its experience; yet these two characteristics inevitably stand in a certain tension with each other. This tension probably underlies what Otto calls the *mysterium fascinans* of the sacred, which leads to a curious ambivalence in the religious attitude—an ambivalence of attraction and flight, of being drawn to the sacred and wanting to escape it. Seen from the standpoint of the individual, the sacred is something emphatically other than himself, yet at the same time affirming him at the very center of his being and integrating him within the order of the cosmos. Mysticism, incidentally, is the most radical solution of this ambivalence, as when the latter is denied in an affimation of the ultimate unity of self and cosmos. But even this solution is not easily attained, as the world literature of mysticism amply demonstrates.

In sum: Both the supernatural and the sacred are specific human experiences, capable of being described (within certain limitations of language) and delineated against other types of experience. Both can especially be delineated against the reality of ordinary, everyday life. Indeed, essential to both is a rupture between this mundane reality and the other realities to which the experiences of the supernatural and the sacred appear to provide an opening. It further appears that the experience of the supernatural is the more fundamental of the two. Originally, the sacred was a manifestation within the reality of the supernatural. But even when the sacred is detached from its original supernatural matrix, a more than faint echo of the latter seems to remain. Thus even modern man, insofar as he has been "emancipated" from the supernatural, is capable of standing in such awe of mundane entities conceived as sacred (such as, for example, the nation-state, or the revolutionary movement, or even science) that the reality of ordinary life seems to him to have been breached.

Religion as Tradition

It thus cannot be emphasized strongly enough that at the core of the phenomenon of religion is a set of highly distinctive experiences. Subsuming what has been said above about the supernatural and the sacred under the common term of "religious experience," it is this latter from which all religion originally derives. Religious experience, however, is not universally and equally distributed among human beings. What is more, even such individuals as have had this experience, with its sense of overpowering certainty, find it very difficult to sustain its subjective reality over time. Religious experience, in consequence, comes to be embodied in traditions, which mediate it to those who have not had it themselves and which institutionalize it for them as well as for those who had.

The embodiment of human experiences in traditions and institutions, of course, is by no means peculiar to religion. On the contrary, it is a general feature of human existence, without which social life would not be possible.[12] The special character of religious experience, however, creates a number of problems. Foremost among these is the root fact that religious experience breaches the reality of ordinary life, while all traditions and institutions are structures *within* the reality of ordinary life. Inevitably, this translation of the experienced contents from one reality to another tends to distort. The translator begins to stammer, or to paraphrase, to leave things out or to add them. His predicament is that of the poet among bureaucrats, or of one who wants to tell of his love at a business meeting. This problem would be there even if the translator had no ulterior motive beyond wanting to tell his experience to those who have not had it. In this case, though, there are ulterior motives of a very specific sort—namely, the motives of those who have acquired a vested interest in the credibility and the authority of the tradition that embodies the translation.

Religious experience posits its own authority, be it in the majesty of the divine address in religions of revelation, or in the overwhelming inner sense of reality of the mystic. As the experience comes to be embodied in a tradition, the authority comes to be transferred to the latter. Indeed, the very quality of sacredness is transferred from that which was experienced *than* (God, gods, or whatever other supernatural entities) in another reality to what is experienced *now* in the mundane reality of ordinary life. In this manner there appear sacred rituals, sacred books, sacred institutions, and sacred functionaries of these institutions. The unutterable is now uttered—and it is *routinely* uttered. The sacred has become a habitual experience; the supernatural has, as it were, become "naturalized."

Once religious experience becomes an institutionalized fact within normal social life, its plausibility is sustained by the same processes that keep plausible any other experience. These processes are, essentially, those of social consensus and social control: The experience is credible because everyone says it is so or acts as if it were, and because various degrees of unpleasantness are imposed on those who would deny it. This obviously constitutes a vast shift in the location of the experience in the individual's consciousness. Thus, for instance, Muhammad accepted the truth of the Koran because it came to him in thunderous voices whose reality was undeniable, in the so-called Night of Glory: "We revealed the Koran on the Night of Qadr [Glory]. Would that you knew what the Night of Qadr is like! Better is the Night of Qadr than a thousand months. On that night the angels and the Spirit by their Lord's leave come down with His decrees. That night is peace, till break of day."[13] Leave aside here the question of how Muhammad himself sustained the reality of that experience in his own mind after the day broke and the voices were silent. But what about the ordinary Muslim today, some thirteen hundred years later? Or, for that matter, the ordinary Muslim a hundred or even ten years later? Angelic visitations were rare even then, and they have become notoriously rare in the meantime. Yet there is no great mystery about the question: The ordinary Muslim today, and for centuries now, accepts the truth of the Koran because he lives in a social milieu in which this acceptance is a routine fact of social life. Empirically speaking, the authority of the Koran and of the entire Muslim tradition now rests on this social foundation.

These considerations could easily be understood as implying a radical anti-institutionalism, according to which all of social life is dismissed as fraud or fiction.[14] That would be a misunderstanding, both in general and with reference to religion in society. The insertion of the supramundane into mundane reality inevitably distorts it, but only by virtue of this distortion can even a faint echo of the original experience be retained amid the humdrum noises of everyday life. The question could be put this way: *How can the nocturnal voices of the angels be remembered in the sobering daytime of ordinary life?* The entire history of religion gives an unambiguous answer: *By incorporating the memory in traditions claiming social authority.* Needless to say, this makes the memory fragile, vulnerable to social change, specifically vulnerable to such changes as weaken the authority of the tradition. But there is no other way for the insights of religious experience to survive in time—or, to use religious language, to survive during those stretches of time when the angels are silent.

A religious tradition, with whatever institutions have grown up around it, exists as a fact in ordinary, everyday reality. It mediates the experience of another reality, both to those who have never had it and to those who have but who are ever in danger of forgetting it. Every tradition is a collective memory.[15] Religious tradition is a collective memory of those moments in which the reality of another world broke into the paramount reality of everyday life. But the tradition not only mediates the religious experience; it also *domesticates* it. By its very nature, religious experience is a standing threat to social order—not just in the sense of this or that sociopolitical status quo but in the more basic sense of the business of living. Religious experience radically relativizes, if it does not devalue altogether, the ordinary concerns of human life. When the angels speak, the business of living pales into insignificance, even irreality. If the angels spoke all the time, the business of living would probably stop completely. No society could survive in the fixed posture of encountering the supernatural. In order for society to survive (and this means, for human beings to go on living), the encounters must be limited, controlled, circumscribed. This domestication of religious experience is one of the most fundamental social as well as psychological functions of religious institutions. Thus religious tradition is also a defense mechanism of the paramount reality, guarding its boundaries against the threat of being overrun by the incursions of the supernatural. Religious tradition keeps at bay those nights of glory that might otherwise engulf all of life. Whatever else it is, religious experience is dangerous. Its dangers are reduced and routinized by means of institutionalization. Religious ritual, for example, assigns the encounters with sacred reality to certain times and places, and puts them under the control of typically prudent functionaries. By the same token, religious ritual liberates the rest of life from the burden of having to undergo these encounters. The individual, thanks to religious ritual, can now go about his ordinary business—making love, making war, making a living, and so on—without being constantly interrupted by messengers from another world. Looking at the matter in this way makes understandable the Latin root of the very word "religion," which is *relegere*—"to be careful." Religious tradition is the careful management of an exceedingly dangerous human experience.[16] In the same process of domestication, the sacred qualities of the experience can be transposed to nonsupernatural entities—first to the religious institutions themselves, subsequently to other institutions (such as the state, the nation, and so forth).

Any human experience that is to be communicated to others and preserved over time must be expressed in symbols.[17] Religious experience is no exception. As soon as the content of such experience is communicated in language, it is included (or, if one prefers, imprisoned) in a specific body of symbolism that has a history and a social location. Thus the Arabic language of the Koran did not (at least as far as the empirical historian or social scientist can determine) fall down from heaven. Rather, it had a particular history, which decisively shaped its character and its capacity to symbolize experience. Muhammad too, as a human being, was shaped by this language, as he was shaped by his location in a particular social context (of region, class, clan, and so forth). With the very first account of his experience, then, the multiple effects of his use of the Arabic language crucially affected the communication process. This does *not* mean that the symbolic apparatus available to Muhammad totally determined his ability to recount his experience. On the contrary, by all the evidence Muhammad was a master of language, maximally adapting the existing language to the requirements of his communication, so that indeed the Koran became in its own right a major influence on the development of the Arabic language. Nevertheless, one can be certain that, even if one assumes that Muhammad's core experience was beyond all human time and place, its communication would have been greatly different if, instead of Arabic, it had taken place in Sanskrit or in Chinese. This assumption can be put more precisely by saying that the relation between religious experience and the symbolic apparatus by means of which it is communicated (and embodied in a tradition) is dialectical—that is, the religious experience and the symbolic apparatus mutually determine each other.

This essentially simple fact, once grasped, precludes one-sided interpretations of the process of religious communication. On the one hand, it precludes the view (as still held, for instance, by orthodox Muslims) that a religious message can totally overpower the body of symbolism by which it is communicated. Put differently, "literal inspiration" is impossible, if for no other reason, because the language of any religious tradition is a *human* language—the product of a human history and the carrier of a vast assemblage of human memories, most of which have nothing whatever to do with religion. On the other hand, though, the same fact precludes the opposite view that religious experience is *nothing but* a reflection of this particular history. This view, of course, is the one that has been expressed in Feuerbach's notion of "projection," which then became of immense importance in its developments by Marx and Freud. It has a very useful kernel of validity: Precisely because religious experience is embodied in human symbols, it can be perceived as a vast symbolization, *ipso facto* "projecting" all the human experiences (including experiences of power relations and of sexuality) that historically produced the symbolic apparatus in question. But that is only looking at one side of the phenomenon. As Muhammad told about the angels, he "projected" the Arabic language, with its full freight of sociohistorical meanings, into the sky. But he did so only because what happened first was his experience that, out of that sky, a totally different reality *projected itself* into the mundane reality in which he, along with everyone else, spoke Arabic. Put differently: *Religion can be understood as a human projection because it is communicated in human symbols. But this very communication is motivated by an experience in which a metahuman reality is injected into human life.*

An important part of any religious tradition is the development of theoretical reflection. This may take the form of the erection of theoretical edifices of vast scope and sophistication, as in the so-called great world religions; or the reflection may be embodied in relatively unsophisticated bodies of myths, legends, or maxims. Quite apart from the root anthropological fact that man is a reflective animal, apparently compelled by his own inner nature to reflect about his experience, a religious tradition must develop reflective thought because of the social requirement of legitimation: Each new generation must have explained to it why things are the way they are in the tradition.[18] As the tradition continues in time, then, there grows with it a body of more or less authoritative accounts and inter-

pretations of the original experience (no matter whether it is
codified in sacred scriptures or not). It is essential for the task
of understanding religion that this aggregate of theoretical
reflection be distinguished from the original experience that
gave rise to it. Anyone with any degree of acquaintance with
religious scholarship knows that this is never easy and sometimes impossible. A classical case of this difficulty is the so-
called quest for the historical Jesus, the problem of uncovering
what "really took place" in Galilee and Jerusalem during those
days—that is, the problem of uncovering the empirical core as
against the overlay of later Christian interpretations (which
of course, already suffuse every page of the New Testament accounts). All the same, the distinction between religious experience and religious reflection is crucial. Otherwise, one of two
errors occurs: Either the inevitably distortive effect of reflection
is overlooked, or the study of religion becomes a history of
theories or "ideas."

To sum up the immediately preceding considerations, the
embodiment of religious experience in traditions and the development of theoretical reflection about the original experience
must be understood both as inevitable and as inevitably distortive. This is a difficulty; but it is also an opportunity, for it
opens up the possibility of going back, as far as possible, to the
core of the experience itself. This is particularly important for
anyone using the modern intellectual disciplines of history and
the social sciences for his understanding of religion. These disciplines are deeply relativizing in their effect—a tradition is understood as the product of multiple historical causes, a theology
as the outcome of this or that socioeconomic conflict, and so
on. More than once, during the last two hundred years or so of
scholarship on religion, the religious phenomenon actually
seemed to disappear beneath these relativizations. It is all the
more useful to recall that religious experience is a constant in

human history. In the words of the Koran once more: "There
is no nation that has not been warned by an apostle."[19]
Beyond all the relativities of history and of mundane reality
as such, it is this core experience, in its various forms, that must
constitute the final objective of any inquiry into the religious
phenomenon. This objective can never be fully attained, both
because of the nature of the empirical evidence and because of
the inquirer's own location within specific sociohistorical relativities. The objective can, at best, be approximated. This
should not be an alibi for not even trying.

Once More: The Modern Situation

For reasons discussed in some detail in the preceding chapter, the modern situation is not conducive to the plausibility of
religious authority. The modern situation, with its closely related aspects of pluralism and secularization, thus puts what
may be called cognitive pressure on the religious thinker. Insofar as the secular worldview of modernity dominates his social
context, the religious thinker is pressured to softpedal if not to
abandon altogether the supernatural elements of his tradition.
In this, of course, he is by no means alone; he shares these pressures with all modern men—intellectuals and nonintellectuals,
those still adhering to a religious tradition and those who no
longer do so. The evidence is not conclusive as to what this
means for religious experience as such—that is, for experience
as it predates reflection about it. Two hypotheses are possible:
One, that modern men have such experience not at all, or at
any rate much less frequently than used to be the case in
earlier times. Or, two, that modern men have such experience
as much as men have ever had it, but that, because of the
delegitimation of the experience by the prevailing worldview,

they hide or deny it (the denial, of course, could be to themselves as well as to others). Whichever hypothesis one deems more probable, it is clear that neither religious experience nor religious reflection can take place in the modern situation with the ease that was possible in earlier periods of history.

In view of the universality and centrality of religious experience in all preceding epochs of history, it is also clear that this suppression or denial has had cataclysmic effects. These have been eloquently caught in Nietzsche's phrase "the death of God," and, as he put it, a world in which God has died has become colder. This coldness has psychological as well as social costs. In Nietzsche's words: "How have we been able to drink up the sea? Who gave us the sponge, with which to erase the horizon? What did we do, when we loosened the earth from its sun? Where does she move now? Where do we move? Away from all suns? Do we not fall perpetually? Forward, sideways, backward, in all directions? Is there still an above and a below? Do we not wander through an infinite nothingness? Are we not haunted by empty space? Has it not become colder?"[20] Needless to say, most modern men have not experienced this disappearance of the divine as violently. For every Nietzsche or Dostoyevsky there are a thousand more or less well-adjusted agnostics, more or less *Angst*-ridden atheists.

All the same, modern man is more alone in the world as a result of the disappearance/denial of religious experience. And modern institutions and societies are also more "alone"— in the sense of being bereft of the reliable legitimations that have always been provided by the sacred symbols derived from religious experience. In consequence, the history of secularization has also been one of displacements and resurgences of these sacred symbols. Because man finds it very difficult to be alone in the cosmos either as an individual or in collectivities, sacredness has been transposed from supernatural to mundane referents. Thus, for example, secular Arab nationalism has been endowed with a sacredness that is no longer plausible in its original Muslim context. But there have also been violent reactions against the repressive secularity of the modern world, in a variety of reaffirmations of religious authority. Thus the Muslim world has been the scene to this day of a score or more of powerful revival movements, reasserting the authority of Islam in the face of all its contemporary challenges. It is not feasible in this book to pursue the sociological and social-psychological implications of either the displacements or the resurgences of religious experience in the modern world, but these phenomena should at least be kept in mind. They too are part of the social context of the contemporary religious thinker.

Assorted Protestant Miseries

Whether or not one agrees with Max Weber's view of the crucial role of the Protestant Reformation and its consequences in the formation of the modern world, one will almost certainly have to agree that, historical causality apart, Protestantism has confronted modernity more massively and for a longer period than any other religious tradition. If Weber was indeed correct, then this special relationship is only what one would expect, since in that case Protestantism was one of the prime shapers of what is now known as modernity. If Weber was wrong or only partially right, then one could look upon the relationship as a curious historical accident, by virtue of which Protestantism happened to develop in those parts of the Western world in which forces of modernity such as capitalism and the industrial revolution made their deepest inroads into society and culture. To the extent that Protestantism has had a special relationship to modernity, it also has had such a relationship to secularization. Thus, throughout the nineteenth century, much of Protestant theology was an ongoing confrontation with various forms of secular thought and secular consciousness. To cite but the most spectacular aspect of this confrontation, it was Protestantism that gave birth to modern biblical scholarship, thus producing the historically unheard-of case of scholars officially accredited as representatives of a religious tradition turning a sharply critical cognitive apparatus against the sacred scriptures of that same tradition. There is a quality of intellectual heroism in this. But be this as it may, no other religious tradition has experienced the challenge of modern secularity in the same degree. Thus, in the same nineteenth century, the general stance of Roman Catholicism toward modern secularity was one of (perhaps just as heroic) defiance. Only in this century, and most especially since the Second Vatican Council, has a comparable confrontation occurred within the Roman Catholic community. Not surprisingly, some of these recent events have appeared as a kind of "Protestantization," with large numbers of Roman Catholic theologians going through the cognitive miseries long familiar to their Protestant confreres.

It follows that the history of Protestant theology is a paradigm for the confrontation of a religious tradition with modernity. Needless to say, this is not necessarily a positive statement. Others can learn from the Protestant paradigm, not necessarily by imitating or reiterating it. The paradigmatic character of Protestantism is the only reason why the discussion of theological options to follow in this book will concentrate on Protestant examples. In other words, if modernity is a cognitive condition, then Protestants have struggled with it for a long time, and the spectacle of this struggle is instructive for others entering into the same condition. In this sense, and in

58   *The Heretical Imperative*

this sense only, one might even adopt Paul Tillich's phrase
"the Protestant era" to designate the modern period in the history of religion.

It also follows from this, incidentally, that the American situation, with its highly peculiar pluralism, constitutes a paradigm
within the paradigm. Talcott Parsons has called America the
"lead society."[21] This description is by no means to be understood as patriotic boastfulness; it simply indicates that specific
modernization forces have gone further in America than any-
where else—and pluralism so above all. In America there has
been a conjuncture of pluralization, "Protestantization," and
secularization, leading to the distinctively American innovation
of the "denomination"—a socioreligious entity which, as Richard Niebuhr showed, has come to accept more or less gracefully
its coexistence with others in a pluralistic situation. John Murray Cuddihy has only recently demonstrated most persuasively
how this American situation has "Protestantized" both Catholics and Jews in a process that, often enough, has had the character of a theological ordeal.[22]

It is interesting in this connection to look at the case of Eastern Orthodoxy in America. The number of Orthodox Christians in America is roughly the same as that of Jews. Yet
Orthodoxy, unlike Judaism, has remained virtually invisible to
others on the American scene, so that Will Herberg, in his by-
now classic study of the American religious "triple melting
pot," could describe the latter simply in terms of "Protestant,
Catholic, Jew," completely ignoring the Orthodox presence.[23]
The reasons for this, of course, are not far to seek. While
American Jews have decisively broken out of ethnic "contain-
ment," American Orthodox have until very recently remained
within a number of ethnic enclaves (Greek, Slavic, and so on).
By the same token, they have thus far escaped the subversive
effects of "Protestantization." But this is changing now. In

1970 the Orthodox Church in America was formed out of what
used to be a branch of the Russian Orthodox Church. In Orthodox ecclesiastical terms, this was nothing all that extraordinary—a proclamation of "autocephaly" by yet another national Orthodox body. In fact, the change has revolutionary
implications, for there now exists, for the first time in America,
an Orthodox church that is no longer defined ethnically, that
uses English as its liturgical language, and that is a self-consciously pan-Orthodox presence on the American religious
scene. One can only speculate at this point what will happen to
these Orthodox Christians, as they move, with their icons and
vestments, onto the centerstage of American religion. One will
be on safe ground if one assumes that they will encounter there
what their predecessors, from Puritans to Jews, have encountered—pluralization and *ipso facto* the existential as well as
cognitive dilemmas of the Protestant paradigm.

But, as has been argued in the preceding chapter, pluralization is today a worldwide phenomenon, a concomitant
(though not always simultaneously so) of the wider process of
modernization. Thus every religious tradition, Western as well
as non-Western, must sooner or later confront it—and *ipso
facto* confront the assorted miseries of the Protestant experience. One may recall here with some irony the triumphalist
universalism of the great Protestant missionary outreach of the
nineteenth century, when the world was to be evangelized
"from Greenland's icy mountains to India's coral strand" (in
the words of Reginald Heber's famous missionary hymn). History is the record of unintended consequences. In a paradoxical
way the world has indeed become "Protestant," though the
brave missionaries that sailed out from Europe and America
with this hymn on their lips would hardly recognize it as such.
Thus K. Sivaraman, in a meeting on interreligious dialogue organized by the all-too-Protestant World Council of Churches,

could speak for "India's coral strand" in these words: "The Hindu in the role of a spokesman and advocate of his religious tradition . . . finds himself facing two different tasks: he has to define and defend the pattern of the faith that he 'represents,' a task in which his 'present' appears little more than his cherished past; he has also to participate in the very process of mediating his past in another process, one in which his past yields imperceptibly to the inescapable presence of the present."[24] "Protestant" language indeed! The situation becomes even more ironic as one observes that Hinduism, along with other non-Western religions, is now energetically returning the compliment of the Protestant missionary outreach—evangelizing Christians and Jews, from California's icy mountains to Long Island's not-so-coral strands. The Protestant disease has become a planetary epidemic.

Three Options for Religious Thought

Three basic options present themselves for religious thought in the pluralistic situation. They will be called here the deductive, reductive, and inductive options, and most of the rest of this book will be devoted to exploring them. But one point should be made immediately: The aforementioned options are typological, and there is no presumption that the typology is exhaustive or that it fits every theological expression on the scene. Now, a good case can be made that anyone who invents yet another typology to fit theologies into should be summarily banished from every decent conversation on these matters—and especially if the typology is threefold and has catchy names! The regrettable fact is that nobody trying to make sense of modern theology (or, for that matter, any other area of intellectual endeavor in which there have been large numbers of different expressions) can *fail* to attempt some sort of typification; otherwise the sheer diversity and complexity of the phenomenon will frustrate any effort at understanding. Once one starts producing typologies, they might as well be threefold and have names that can be remembered. All this is just another way of saying that Max Weber's caveat on what he called "ideal types" applies here: No typology exists as such in the world; it is always an intellectual construct. Thus it can never be found in pure form, and there will always be cases that do not fit into it. But this does not matter. The typology will be useful to the extent that it helps to discriminate between empirically available cases, and in consequence to make possible both understanding and explanation. The usefulness of the typology, then, can be established only as it is actually applied, and the antitypologist is hereby requested to control his irritation for the moment.

The deductive option is to reassert the authority of a religious tradition in the face of modern secularity. The tradition thus having been restored to the status of a datum, of something given a priori, it is then possible to deduce religious affirmations from it at least more or less as was the norm in premodern times. As will be elaborated in the next chapter, there are different ways to make such a reassertion of traditional authority. Whatever the way, the individual who takes this option experiences himself as responding to a religious reality that is sovereignly independent of the relativizations of his own sociohistorical situation. In a Christian context (it would be the same in a Jewish or Muslim one), he confronts once more the majestic authority that derives from the words *"Deus dixit"*—God speaking once more through the scriptures and the ongoing proclamation of their message, thus continuing to speak to contemporary men as he spoke to the prophets and messengers to whom he revealed himself when the tradition began. The deductive option has the cognitive advantage of once more providing religious reflection with objective criteria of validity. The major disadvantage is the difficulty of sustaining the subjective plausibility of such a procedure in the modern situation.

The reductive option is to reinterpret the tradition in terms of modern secularity, which in turn is taken to be a compelling necessity of participating in modern consciousness. There are, of course, degrees of doing this. Thus, for instance, anyone using methods of modern historical scholarship is secularizing the tradition by this very fact, since these scholarly tools are themselves the products of a modern secular consciousness. The reductive option, however, is marked by something more radical than the employment of this or that modern intellectual tool. It is, as it were, an exchange of authorities: The authority of modern thought or consciousness is substituted for the authority of the tradition, the *Deus dixit* of old replaced by an equally insistent *Homo modernus dixit*. In other words, modern consciousness and its alleged categories become the only criteria of validity for religious reflection. These criteria are also given an objective status, insofar as those who take this option tend to have very definite ideas as to what is and what is not "permissible" to say for a modern man. Taking this option opens up a cognitive program, by which affirmations derived from the tradition are systematically translated into terms "permissible" within the framework of modern secularity. The major advantage of this option is that it reduces cognitive dissonance, or seems to do so. The major disadvantage is that the tradition, with all its religious contents, tends to disappear or dissolve in the process of secularizing translation.

The inductive option is to turn to experience as the ground of all religious affirmations—one's own experience, to whatever extent this is possible, and the experience embodied in a particular range of traditions. This range may be of varying breadth —limited minimally to one's own tradition, or expanded maximally to include the fullest available record of human religious history. In any case, induction means here that religious traditions are understood as bodies of evidence concerning religious experience and the insights deriving from experience. Implied in this option is a deliberately empirical attitude, a weighing and assessing frame of mind—not necessarily cool and dispassionate, but unwilling to impose closure on the quest for religious truth by invoking any authority whatever—not the authority of this or that traditional *Deux dixit*, but also not the authority of modern thought or consciousness. The advantage of this option is its open-mindedness and the freshness that usually comes from a nonauthoritarian approach to questions of truth. The disadvantage, needless to say, is that open-mindedness tends to be linked to open-endedness, and this frustrates the deep religious hunger for certainty. The substitution of hypothesis for proclamation is profoundly uncongenial to the religious temperament.

Despite this disadvantage (one, as will be argued later, that need not be lethal), this book is based on the conviction that the third option is the only one that promises both to face and to overcome the challenges of the modern situation. This contention too, of course, will have to be elaborated. But it should be clear now why the elaboration in this chapter of the relations between religious experience, tradition, and reflection was necessary. The inductive option cannot even be considered unless these distinctions are made. The relativizations of modernity are irresistible if religion is taken as nothing but a body of theoretical propositions. In that event, the exchange of one plausibility structure for another must necessarily be followed by an exchange of cognitive authorities. Or, if one prefers, secular dogmatics takes over where traditional religious dogma is no longer plausible. The distinctions made in this chapter, on the other hand, make possible a different avenue of questioning, a search for the experience that lies behind or beneath this or that religious tradition, this or that body of theoretical propositions produced by religious reflection. The inductive option entails the taking of a deliberately naïve attitude before the accounts of human experiences in this area, trying as far as possible, and without dogmatic prejudices, to grasp the core contents of these experiences. The inductive option is, in this sense, phenomenological. Its naïveté is the same that Husserl suggested in his famous marching order for philosophers: *"Zurück zu den Sachen!"*—loosely translated as "Back to things as they are!"[25]

The inductive option is rooted in the modern situation and its heretical imperative. Indeed, it is the fullest acceptance of that imperative. But it is not part of the option to elevate modernity to the status of a new authority, and it is this absolutely fundamental point that distinguishes it from the reductive option. The experiences of modernity are part of the evidence too—no more, no less. The attitude toward modernity, then, is one neither of condemnation nor of celebration. If anything, it is one of detachment. This attitude provides some safeguards both against reactionary nostalgia and against revolutionary overenthusiasm. It is not a terribly easy attitude. All too often the inductive approach ends in reductionism, or alternatively its frustrations lead to surrender to the old certainties. Yet it affords a quite distinctive experience of inner liberation (which is perhaps itself to be located on the margins of religious experience proper).

The turn from authority to experience as the focus of religious thought is, of course, by no means new. It has been the hallmark of Protestant theological liberalism at least since Friedrich Schleiermacher. It is not necessary to approve every aspect of Schleiermacher's thought in order to admire the daring with which he executed this turn. Nor is it necessary to go along with every twist in the long history of this school of thought in order to identify with its basic intention. In identifying with the inductive option, however, this book is also identified with the basic intention of Protestant theological liberalism—without any apology at all. It should be recalled here once more, though, what was said above about the Protestant paradigm. To the same extent that modernity has become a general context for religious reflection, the Protestant efforts to cope with modernity are of general interest. The inductive option, while it has been a central motif of Protestant theological liberalism, is certainly not an option limited to Protestants. Just as the restoration of traditional authority and secularization are options for Catholics, Jews, Muslims, Buddhists, and any other groups that have entered the modern world (or, more accurately, on whom the modern world has descended), the Protestant cognitive exercises in the face of modernity will show themselves to be highly relevant for anyone concerned with the modern predicament of religion. To paraphrase Pius XI, "Today we are all Protestants." This statement is no ethnocentric boast. It is a threat, a lament, but also a hesitant expression of hope.

3

The Deductive Possibility: Reaffirming Tradition

FIVE TIMES A DAY, in Muslim communities from the Atlantic Ocean to the China Sea, the call to prayer is sounded from a thousand minarets. It marks the passage of the hours and, by the same token, the passage of days that make up an individual's biography. And it ensures, in the most palpable way possible, that the tradition it proclaims serves as the continuous background of the human lives that take place in its hearing. In a community as yet untouched by the relativizing forces of modernization, as was argued earlier, the tradition thus proclaimed possesses a taken-for-granted authority. The subjective correlate of this authority is inner certainty. As the proclamation of God's majesty and of Muhammad's prophethood is issued from the minaret, there takes place an inner antiphony in the minds of those who hear it: *"Yes, it is so, and it can be no other."* Indeed, it may be said that this antiphony between external and internal affirmation is the very essence of existence in a traditional society.

Modernization introduces a corrosive dissonance into this antiphony. The external affirmation goes on, in most instances, but the inner response becomes discontinuous, hesitant, or uncertain. The response now becomes something like this: "Yes, I have heard this before; but it *could* be other; is it really so?" Nevertheless, for large numbers of people in modernized situations there remains the memory of moments when, in the confrontation with the old authority, there has been that inward assent and the concomitant certainty. Typically, these will be moments in childhood or early youth, enveloped in the nostalgia that such moments tend to have. This memory serves as the psychological substratum for any subsequent reaffirmations of the tradition. It allows such reaffirmations to have the subjective plausibility of a return to one's own biographical roots. There is then a restoration of the antiphony, doubly joyous because of the interval during which it was interrupted: "Yes, I can now say it *again*; it is so, and it can be no other."

This could be the case, say, of an individual from a Muslim country who, having spent many years as a student in the West, comes home and once again hears the call from the minaret. The experience is prototypical, and similar cases can easily be described, *mutatis mutandis*, for Christians, Jews, Hindus, or individuals belonging to any other tradition. What is more, though, the same experience can be collective. Thus entire groups of people may return (if you will, may "come home") to a reaffirmation of tradition. On the level of the ordinary man-in the-street, there is then the phenomenon variously called "revivalism," "nativism," or "neotraditionalism." In contemporary Turkey, for example, there has been such a phenomenon in recent years, a mass movement of powerful Islamic resurgence coming after many years of Kemalist secularism. The same phenomenon can also occur on the level of intellectual life, in which case the term "neo-orthodoxy" is often used. The tradition is then reaffirmed in theory as well as in religious and sociopolitical practice. The contemporary Muslim world is again rich in examples of this kind. However, whether for the man-in-the-street or the intellectual, there is a built-in problem for these reaffirmations. The problem is contained in the insidious connotations of the little prefix "neo." The tradition is affirmed *anew*, after an interval when it was *not* affirmed. The problem is, quite simply, that it is very difficult to forget this interval. The individual who says, anew, that "it can be no other" remembers the time when he thought that it *could* be other. This is why neotraditional and neo-orthodox movements come on with particular vehemence. Typically, they are a very noisy lot. No wonder: The recollections of that interval when the tradition was less than certain must be drowned out.

The Case of Protestant Neo-orthodoxy

The history of Protestant theology in this century is highly instructive in this regard. To repeat what was said earlier about Protestantism: More than any other religious tradition, and for a longer period of time, Protestantism has been grappling with the relativizing forces of modernity. This is why the Protestant case can be viewed as paradigmatic. If modernization is an ordeal, then Protestants have been undergoing it in a vicarious fashion for all the other traditions; indeed, one is almost tempted to evoke the biblical image of the "suffering servant" here. Be this as it may, non-Protestants and non-Christians, who are more recent arrivals in this particular battle front, would do well to heed the Protestant experience.

The nineteenth century, in the history of Protestant theology, has very convincingly been called the age of Schleiermacher.[1] The latter saw his mission in a defense and reformulation of Christian faith in the face of the onslaught of modern skepticism. He was the true father of theological liberalism, so recognized by both its proponents and critics. By the same token, he was the father of what has been called here the inductive approach, at least in its contemporary form. The bedrock of his theological enterprise was a grounding of Christian faith in a more general human phenomenon of religious experience, of which Christianity was one case in point and in his opinion, of course, the most elevated one. Everything that followed Schleiermacher was either a development or a refutation of this position, which amounted to a Copernican revolution in theological thinking. In a later part of this book closer attention will be paid to this theoretical enterprise. For the moment it should only be stressed again that, if one grants the sociological argument in the preceding two chapters, Schleiermacher's turn to experience was not eccentric or arbitrary but an almost necessary consequence of the modern challenge to traditional authority. The turning inward of religious reflection must be seen in the context of the social and *ipso facto* psychological weakening of outward authority. Put differently, the quest for certainty on the basis of subjective insights is the result of the frustration of this quest by what is socially available as objective reality-definitions.

Even the observer with no personal stake in Protestantism will have to admire the intellectual integrity of some of those who participated in this drama. The history of biblical scholarship, in its modern historical-critical form an overwhelmingly Protestant creation, provides many examples of this.[2] One example, of virtually heroic proportions, is Julius Wellhausen, who inaugurated the application of modern methods of historical scholarship to the Pentateuch. There is a touching episode in Wellhausen's life. He had been teaching for many years on the theological faculty of the University of Greifswald and found it increasingly difficult to do so in a situation where it was his duty to prepare students for the Protestant ministry.

The results of his scholarship, it seems, were not conducive to inspiring fervor in the pulpit. Plunged into a crisis of conscience, Wellhausen wrote a letter to the Prussian minister of culture, describing his dilemma and asking for a transfer to the philosophical faculty. The request was refused, and Wellhausen had to go to another university to have his way in this matter.[3] Others stayed in the theological context, continuing to practice a scholarly discipline that shook the foundations of their own faith as well as that of their students—and attempting, by whatever theoretical means available, to reconcile this conflict honestly and without a sacrifice of intellect. Non-Protestants, especially Catholics, have followed in their wake since that time. But there is no comparable case in the history of religion before the Protestant one in which people from within a tradition to which they were personally committed turned upon it the full arsenal of critical scholarship and let the theological chips fly where they might.

The nineteenth century in Protestant theology ended not in 1900 but in 1918.[4] The First World War provided the shock that brought about this end, as it ended so many other things in European culture. And, when all is said and done, the nature of the shock is not hard to describe: Modernity, it was now felt, had not fulfilled its promises, had perhaps even been a great illusion. Whatever else it had been, the liberal theology of the nineteenth century had been optimistic, progress-minded, favorably disposed to the world in which it found itself. In this, of course, it was no different from other expressions of thought. This was, after all, the climactic age of bourgeois civilization, seemingly secure and assured of ongoing improvement, not only in Europe but throughout the world. There were dissenters from this bourgeois triumphalism (one may mention Kierkegaard, Nietzsche, and Dostoyevsky in this connection—all of whom, significantly, came into their own only after the era against which they protested had ended), but they remained on the margin of the cultural and intellectual scene. It is possible to say, quite simply, that the liberal theological enterprise derived its plausibility in large part from the safe bourgeois world that was its social context. Just because the latter was so safe, individuals such as the aforementioned biblical scholars could, as it were, afford their daring intellectual adventures. This safe world collapsed once and for all in that war, which may well be described as a collective suicide of European civilization. What is more, the fact of this collapse did not take long to sink in. It was visible right away, starkly and frighteningly, as were its moral and intellectual consequences. Not surprisingly, this was especially so in central Europe, dominated by that German culture that was now linked to a nation that had been catastrophically defeated.

It was in this territory, almost immediately after the war, that there erupted that movement which later, especially in America, came to be called "neo-orthodoxy."[5] Perhaps it is sociologically significant that it began on the borders of Germany but not in Germany itself. In any case, there is no dispute that its central, indeed overpowering figure was the Swiss theologian Karl Barth. If the period that ended in 1918 was the age of Schleiermacher in Protestant theology, then surely the period between the two wars (and perhaps the first few years following the Second World War) was the age of Barth. In every way, theoretically as well as practically, and even in its emotional tones, Barth's theology constituted a violent refutation of what had preceded it. It was, at its very core, a thunderous *no* to all the assumptions and achievements of Protestant theological liberalism. The thunder broke, deafeningly, with the publication of one book—Barth's commentary on Paul's Epistle to the Romans. It first appeared in 1918, then again in a greatly revised edition in 1921, and it immediately created a storm of controversy. Barth, later on, commented on this by using a richly evocative image: It was, he said, like a man climbing up inside a church steeple in the dark; stumbling up the steps, he clutches for support, only to discover that he has taken hold of the bell rope—and, before he realizes what is happening, he has caused the bell to ring out with a mighty boom.

Protestant neo-orthodoxy (or "dialectical theology," as it was called at the beginning in the German-speaking countries) became a movement very soon.[6] A circle of other individuals formed around Barth and found their principal medium of expression in the new journal *Zwischen den Zeiten* ("Between the Times"); some of these individuals continued to stay close to Barth, others went their separate ways later on. When Barth accepted a university appointment in Germany, the center of the movement shifted to that country. This became of paramount importance in the 1930s with the rise of Nazism to power. In terms of the plausibility of different theological positions two dates are of primary significance here: 1914, when a group including most of the great names of German liberal theology signed a "Manifesto of the Intellectuals," enthusiastically endorsing the German war effort—an event, as Barth explained, that decisively shook his confidence in his erstwhile teachers and led him to think along radically novel ways. And 1934, when a group of Protestant theologians and churchmen, many of them under Barth's influence, issued the "Theological Declaration of Barmen," repudiating the then widely promulgated idea that the Nazi revolution had revelatory import for Christians. This latter event, for many, remained decisive in showing the capacity of Barthian theology to stand up to the pretensions of the modern age. In other words, the *no* of neo-orthodoxy to accommodation with the secular world became more plausible than ever when that world took the form of Nazism, and even people who otherwise might not have been attracted to Barthianism were attracted in consequence of its opposition to Nazism. Insofar as there was resistance to Nazism in German Protestantism, neo-orthodoxy (not necessarily in its purely Barthian form; there were also, for instance, Lutheran forms) was the ideology of that resistance. This gave it, and justly so, an aura of heroism that was not irrelevant to its plausibility. Conversely, it may be said that the decline of neo-orthodoxy after World War II had much to do with the inevitable fading of this aura.[7]

Obviously the extremely intricate history of these developments cannot be traced here. Equally preposterous would be any attempt to delineate or discuss the majestic Barthian opus. What can be done is only this: The basic methodological assumptions of Barth's theology will be analyzed as offering a model for the cognitive strategies employed by Protestant neo-orthodoxy—and, if the foregoing argument holds, for the cognitive strategies available, in principle, to non-Protestant or for that matter non-Christian neo-orthodoxies. Barth was a brilliant, highly dynamic thinker, and his theology changed in a number of important areas in the course of his life. It is probably fair to say, however, that his basic methodological approach remained the same. In any case, for the present purpose this approach will be taken as found in the first two half-volumes of Barth's monumental *Church Dogmatics*. The extent to which Barth changed his mind about these propositions at a later date may be left to the experts, as may the question to what extent his own work was or remained faithful to these methodological assumptions. All that matters here is that the opening portions of the *Church Dogmatics* provide a methodological statement

of unusual lucidity; the contention here is that this statement
may be viewed as a model for a much broader array of theological possibilities in the modern situation.

"A Flake-like Thing on the Face of the Wilderness"

Barth's entire work is dominated by an overwhelming sense
of confrontation with the Word of God: The God of Christian
faith is a God who speaks, and the only adequate response on
the part of men is listening in obedience. This Word of God,
originally spoken to the prophets and witnesses of the past, is
contained in the Holy Scriptures and is ever again made alive
in the preaching of the church. Theology, or any form of
specifically Christian thought, can have no other starting point
than this same Word of God. It is an intellectual enterprise,
may even be a scholarly one, but it is finally nothing but the
collective reflection of the church about this Word of God that
has been entrusted to the church. Thus theology cannot bring
any external criteria to this Word (such as might be derived
from philosophy or the empirical sciences); the Word itself
provides the criteria for its interpretation; the Word is *given* to
the Christian thinker, in the double sense of being the *datum*
that precedes all reflection and of being the *gift* of God.[8]
Theological reflection presupposes faith, which in turn is
obedience to God's call. Thus theology, although it is an intellectual activity, is itself a prolonged act of faith. Such faith,
however, is not based on a free decision by man but rather is
the consequence of God's grace.[9] It follows that all attempts, as
those characteristic of liberal theology, to find avenues of approach to God's Word from the side of man are doomed to
failure: There is no way from man to God; there is only the way

that God has already gone in speaking to man.[10] Put differently, man can know nothing about God, except what God has revealed about himself. The root fault of liberal theology has been that it takes unbelief far too seriously. The proper task of theological reflection is not to meet the arguments of unbelief or to produce arguments of its own on behalf of belief but to clarify the contents of the revelation that has already been given to faith.[11]

Thus it is an altogether wrong question if one asks, "How can man know God's Word?" There is no possible answer to this question. Rather, one must ask, "How do these men, those who have faith, know God?" The reality of God's Word—in its original revelation, in the Scriptures, and in the proclamation (kerygma) of the church—is founded in nothing but itself, posits itself, and cannot be arrived at by any "method" whatsoever. Those who hear the Word of God in the church already stand in this reality. God knows who they are. There is also no answer to the question of how anyone can get himself into this position of being able to hear the Word of God and to confront its reality. Of course this hearing of the Word of God is also an event in time, a human experience, which can be studied as such by the historian or other empirical observers. But nothing that can be discovered by such investigations will bring anyone even one bit closer to the revelatory reality. The error of liberal theology, from Schleiermacher on, and the error of all modern thought ever since Descartes, was to think that there is some innate capacity of man to experience the divine. There is no such capacity. Only the Word itself gives the capacity to affirm it.[12]

The theological revolution proposed here is made clearly visible in this understanding of the place of experience. The liberal use of human experience, especially religious experience, as the starting point of theological reflection is vehemently rejected.

Experience of God's Word is indeed possible, but only by means of this Word. Every human response to the Word is exclusively determined by God's grace; none of it based on man's self-determination. Thus the experience of God's Word cannot be rooted in any anthropologically given quality—not in will, or conscience, or emotionality, or reason. The list effectively eliminates the major "methods" that have been suggested as avenues to faith. The experience can only be brought about by faith. Nevertheless, the experience can include a sense of certainty. That certainty too, however, is a gift of grace, and it will always be a "trembling certainty."[13] Man, in any of his natural qualities, is incapable of hearing or experiencing the Word of God; his "capacitation" to hear and experience is the gist of what faith is all about.[14] Put differently, faith is not a human "possibility."[15] It happens if and when God wants it to happen. The perfect metaphor for this is the biblical story of God letting the manna fall from heaven: That too was not rooted in any innate capacity of the people of Israel, nor could they bring it about by any "method" of manna-getting, nor could the event be described as one of many "possibilities" open to them.[16] Indeed, the biblical account states that the Israelites did not know what the manna was until Moses told them: "In the evening quails came up and covered the camp; and in the morning dew lay round about the camp. And when the dew had gone up, there was on the face of the wilderness a fine, flake-like thing, fine as hoarfrost on the ground. When the people of Israel saw it, they said to one another, 'What is it?' For they did not know what it was. And Moses said to them, 'It is the bread which the Lord has given you to eat'" (Exodus 16:13–15, RSV). This story, in Barth's view, contains just about everything there is to be said about faith, and about all alleged avenues toward faith.

The events in which God reveals himself are very specific. And, of course, to Christian faith the decisive event, a highly specific one, is the self-revelation of God in Jesus Christ. The second half-volume of the *Church Dogmatics* begins with the lapidary sentence: "According to the Holy Scripture God's revelation takes place in that God's Word became a man, so that this man was God's Word. The incarnation of the eternal Word, Jesus Christ, is God's revelation."[17] The particularistic character of Christian faith could not be reaffirmed more starkly. Thus the entire section that follows this sentence is entitled "Jesus Christ—The Objective Reality of Revelation." This fierce particularism (or christocentrism, which amounts to the same thing here) is central to Barth's position and very important to keep in mind. It determines Barth's understanding both of human religion in general and of the various non-Christian religions.

Barth allows that, from the viewpoint of the historian, Christian faith can be seen as yet another case of human religion. But this cannot be the viewpoint of the Christian theologian. The latter may, indeed, even speak of Christianity as the "true religion," but this usage is finally misleading. Christian faith, because of its aforementioned character, is something quite different from any form of human religion. Indeed, as God's revelation is the abolition and conclusion (*Aufhebung*) of religion, so, in the perspective of faith, all human religion is seen to be unbelief and disobedience.[18] Because of this radical counterposition of faith and religion, Barth is of the opinion that the Christian theologian can be very relaxed indeed in confronting the various relativizations of religion brought about by historical scholarship and other modern empirical disciplines: None of them can touch the faith in Jesus Christ; all they do touch is varieties of religion which faith has already relativized (and *aufgehoben*) long before the advent of modernity. Thus Barth can even write a very sympathetic, basically approving, little study of the thought of Feuerbach, the father of Marxian and Freudian atheism, who looked upon religion as nothing but a "projection" of human realities.[19]

Perhaps the most fascinating passage in the *Church Dogmatics* is a long note in which Barth discusses the similarities between Protestant Christianity and the so-called Pure Land schools of Japanese Buddhism.[20] These are a development of Mahayana Buddhism into what a number of scholars have called a "religion of grace," in which any personal efforts toward salvation (as through the ascetic disciplines dear to Buddhist monasticism) are surrendered in favor of faith in the saving power of Amida, one of the great bodhisattvas (that is, one who has attained Buddhahood, but who, out of compassion for suffering humanity, delays his entry into nirvana in order to bring about the salvation of other beings). The similarities between this "religion of grace" and Protestantism are indeed striking—to the point that Catholic missionaries coming to Japan in the seventeenth century reported that they had found there a strange variety of the Lutheran heresy! Far from being disturbing, these similarities, according to Barth, are actually "providential": For the case of Pure Land Buddhism shows more clearly than anything else that the truth of Christianity cannot be established from any of its characteristics, cannot, that is, be made credible by any "method" of rational or empirical assessment. Rather, the truth of Christianity is accessible only through the self-revelation of the Word of God, as grasped in faith. What is more, the difference between Christianity and other religion (more precisely, any religion) lies, simply and exclusively, in the *name* of Jesus Christ. In this scandalous particularity, of course, Barth goes

back directly to the New Testament: "And there is salvation in
no one else for there is no other name under heaven given
among men by which we must be saved" (Acts 4:12, RSV).

Critique of Leaping

Barth was a thinker of enormous force and brilliance, and as
such must be taken on his own terms rather than as a type if
justice is to be done to his thought. But such is not the present
purpose. Quite apart from his unique qualities, Barth does represent a much broader intellectual possibility, the one that has
been aptly called neo-orthodoxy. His thought is indeed the
most important example of this possibility in the Christian
context of the twentieth century. And as such it is very instructive.

*Neo-orthodoxy is the reaffirmation of the objective authority
of a religious tradition after a period during which that authority had been relativized and weakened.* Precisely because the
objective status of the tradition has been questioned, it must
now be reasserted with great force. The period between the
original proclamation of the tradition and its reproclamation in
the present ("between the times" indeed) must, so to speak,
be "forgotten." Once more the individual is to confront the
thunderous self-certification of the revelatory message. If this
feat is actually accomplished, the cognitive gain is obvious:
After a period of doubt and compromise there will once more
be certainty. What is more, if the objectivity of the tradition
has actually been reconstructed, then the old cognitive formula
of deducing propositions from it can once more be employed.
This is why neo-orthodoxy is here referred to as the deductive
possibility. It should be emphasized that this in no way implies
an arid scholasticism or an unreflective intellectual stance; if

such an implication were intended, Barth would not have been taken as an example. Rather this implies precisely what Barth himself so eloquently stated: Once more theology returns to its source and derives all its propositions from the revelation, the "Word of God," assumed to be given there.

Any critique of neo-orthodoxy must begin with the obvious question of how an individual manages to get himself into this position—the position, that is, of standing under the "Word of God" in this manner. Barth, as has been noted, rejects the question. Faith, he insists, is not to be attained by any human "method" whatever; it is given; it is not "mediated" by any human experience or action. There is something grandiose about this answer. One can greatly admire it. One can also, with all respect, disbelieve it.

Both the historian and the sociologist, confronted with assertions like this, will always ask the impolite question "Says who?" The answers are usually embarrassing as well as illuminating. Nobody is born as a theoretician, not even a great thinker like Barth. In his case, it is lucidly clear how he managed to get himself into the position of saying what he said from 1918 on—there were all the "mediations" of his situation in time and place, beginning with the great disappointment of 1914, when the elite of liberal theology in Germany succumbed to the nationalistic orgy of the war. Put simply, Barth asserts that the position of having faith is unmediated; against this assertion, a whole array of mediating circumstances can be enumerated. But that is not all. He also asserts that there is no method by which faith is to be attained; against this assertion, and thus against his own self-definition, a method can be pointed to and described.

The method is that of Kierkegaard; it is the method of what the latter called the "leap of faith." What is more, that method is peculiarly determined by the situation of modernity.[21] It can be described rather simply: In the situation of doubt and despair, the individual confronts once again the message embodied in the tradition and, by a wrenching existential effort, jumps into the position of saying, "Yes, I believe." The individual who does this was called the "knight of faith" by Kierkegaard. And the latter, of course, was greatly impressed by the subjective character of this feat, to the point that the climactic assertion of his theoretical method is that "truth is subjectivity."[22] The "dialectic," in Kierkegaard's thought, is between that totally unprotected subjectivity and the objective reality that faith affirms. It is very interesting to see what happened to this dialectic in Barth's thought. As he himself often confessed, he was greatly influenced by Kierkegaard in his early thinking. Yet, as the Barthian opus unfolds, the Kierkegaardian and generally the "existentialist" starting point recedes more and more. Despite the fact that Barthianism continued to be called "dialectical theology" in the German-speaking world, it is hard to find this dialectic in its later stages. No wonder: The more the *given* character of the "Word of God" is asserted— and this means precisely its objectivity—the more the subjective history of *how one came to find it* must be suppressed. Kierkegaard is the specter that haunts the Barthian opus. It is no disrespect to say that Barth had to repress that specter; such repression was a cognitive imperative of his method. Put simply, neo-orthodoxy asserts that its faith is given; the critique of neo-orthodoxy must assert that, on the contrary, this faith is found by certain individuals as a result of empirically available efforts. Of all the mediations that Barth rejects, his own can be embarrassingly pinpointed: It is an effort of the will. Put differently, neo-orthodoxy is the result of a decision—the decision to believe again. For reasons that have been detailed in the preceding chapters, such "decisionism" is a peculiar characteristic of reflective thought in the modern situation.[23]

Once the subjective roots of neo-orthodoxy, its methodological preconditions, are uncovered, the neo-orthodox claim to objectivity is put in question. But then one must also ask a further question, a very simple one: Assuming that these affirmations can be made in the wake of a "leap of faith"—*why should one leap in the first place?*

Kierkegaard answered this question with unassailable frankness and in great detail. Indeed, his answer (though originally given in Danish) has naturalized a German word into the language of college-educated Americans: One leaps out of *Angst*. Human existence is perceived as a welter of anxiety and miseries; the "leap of faith" is the one way out of despair. This perception of the human condition is, of course, the root perception of any form of post-Kierkegaardian existentialism. If that perception is granted, it is indeed plausible to leap. If it is not granted, or even if it is qualified by more optimistic considerations, the plausibility is much lessened. Individuals have probably always differed in their susceptibility to *Angst*. One man's occasion for despair is another's quite tolerable situation. More importantly, though, the plausibility of leaping into faith has *social* determinants. In the language used earlier, there is a sociologically analyzable plausibility structure for both the Kierkegaardian perception of the world and the Kierkegaardian solution to the problem posed by this perception. Undoubtedly there are biographical and historical factors to be considered. Thus a "man from the underground" (Kierkegaard can certainly be called by that Dostoyevskyan title) is more likely to despair and then to leap than a well-adjusted, even-tempered member of the Copenhagen bourgeoisie. And it was more plausible to leap into neo-orthodoxy in Germany in the 1930s than the 1950s. But the basic contention here is that the comprehensive plausibility structure for this type of "decisionism" is the modern situation as such. Modernity, as such, even for well-adjusted individuals living in reasonably happy times, produces the *Angst* of finding oneself in a world without certainties. That is quite enough, all by itself, to make various forms of faith-leaping plausible.

There is, however, a further question that arises once one doubts the neo-orthodox believer's claim that he is where he is through no fault of his own: Granting that there is a reason to leap, *where should one leap?* Or, to put the same question in religious terms: Granting a motive to reaffirm the authority of religious tradition, *which tradition is one going to affirm?*

This question, of course, recalls the earlier discussion of pluralism as a key ingredient of the modern situation. It is not clear whether Kierkegaard ever confronted the possibility of leaping into any faith other than the Christian one. One may surmise that, in the Copenhagen of his day, any such possibility would have been rather abstract. Be this as it may, Barth was clearly troubled by this question, as indicated in the fascinating passage on Pure Land Buddhism cited above. The neo-orthodox claim must necessarily rest on the assumption that the "Word of God" is *uniquely* given in the particular revelatory tradition that is reaffirmed. From Schleiermacher on, of course, liberal Protestant theology was greatly troubled by what it called "the problem of the other religions." In various ways the attempt was made to show that Christianity was the true religion, or at least the one closest to truth, because of its alleged cognitive or moral superiority. In retrospect, many of these attempts are less than convincing. Thus, for example, more recent scholarship has pretty much demolished the liberal assumptions about the uniqueness of the ethics of Jesus.[24] All the same, liberal theology grappled with the problem. Barth refused to grapple. The uniqueness of Christian faith is *given* along with all its other affirmations. The revelation proclaims itself as being unique ("no other name under heaven . . ."), and this uniqueness becomes part and parcel of the faith that reappropriates the traditional contents.

In Barth's case, this position led to an often violent and arrogant-sounding attitude toward the non-Christian religions. D. T. Niles, a Christian theologian from India who was (understandably) greatly concerned with the "problem of the other religions," recounts a conversation with Barth in which the latter stated (as he did extensively in the *Church Dogmatics*), "Other religions are just unbelief." Niles asked Barth how many Hindus he had ever met. None, Barth replied. "How then do you know that Hinduism is unbelief?" Niles asked. Barth answered, "A priori."[25] It is almost certainly unfair to take the seeming arrogance of this answer at face value. It must be understood in the context of Barth's thought, which asserts that Christianity qua religion is also unbelief—indeed, just because of its closeness to the "Word of God," Christianity as a human religious phenomenon is the most dangerous unbelief of all. For Barth, as noted above, *all* human religion is unbelief, and Christian faith is not to be subsumed under the category of religion. But the violence of Barth's repudiation of the problem posed by the non-Christian religions is a necessary consequence of his method. As soon as that problem is allowed into the theological universe of discourse, the a priori objectivity of the neo-orthodox position begins to collapse. For at that very moment it is no longer clear in which direction—that is, toward which tradition—one is supposed to leap.

The point could be made rather devastatingly if anyone took the trouble of translating some key passages of the *Church Dogmatics* into Muslim terms; the exercise could also be done for other religions, including Hinduism, but the Muslim case is particularly instructive, because of the proclamatory ("kerygmatic") character of the Muslim understanding of revelation. Very little in Barth's basic methodological assumptions would have to be changed. Here too the "Word of God," as given in the Koran, confronts the individual with unswerving, majestic certainty. Here too all human objections, all "mediations," are revealed to be as naught. Indeed, one of the worst sins in the Muslim view is any attempt to "mediate" between God and man; there is no "intermediary" except the revelation that God himself has initiated. To say otherwise is, in the Muslim view, to be guilty of *shirk*, the heresy that associates God with others and thus denies his radical uniqueness. It might be observed in passing that Islam perceives Christianity precisely as such a heresy, which is why the Koran reiterates that God has no one besides him or like unto himself, has no "companions," and has not begotten anyone. God's revelation, as contained in the Koran, confronts the individual as an unshakable objective fact. Before this fact the individual can do nothing but submit, and it is from this submission (*'aslama*, in Arabic) that Islam derives its name. And, as in the case of Calvinism, the Muslim view is that God, in his infinite wisdom, has predestined who will make this submission and who will not. In the words of the Koran, "Had your Lord pleased, all the people of the earth would have believed in Him. . . . None can have faith except by the will of Allah."[26]

Barth's paradigm for his understanding of faith, the falling of God's manna from heaven on the undeserving people of Israel, applies just as well to the descent of the Koran from heaven on the sacred night of Qadr. The individual who submits to this revelation and affirms it in the Muslim creed performs an act of faith that, in each point, is fully comparable to Barth's. The individual who performs that act after a period of doubts and uncertainty—that is, the Muslim neo-orthodox theologian—is then capable of an equally comparable sense of coming home to a trembling certainty. In the words of a contemporary Muslim writer (at the end of a highly instructive book, in which the author argues with an atheist friend who embodies all the doubts of modern man), "Then I read the Koran. . . . I read the life of this man [Muhammad] and what he did, and I told myself: Yes, he is a prophet! It is impossible that he should be anything else! This wonderful universe can have no other author than the omnipotent God of whom the Koran speaks."[27] *Deus dixit*, in a slightly altered version: "There is no god but Allah, and Muhammad is his prophet!"

An individual to whom these conflicting claims to absolute authority are subjectively accessible (and there are many such individuals today) must ask himself, quite simply, why one should have *this* faith rather than *that*, why one should be a Christian rather than a Muslim, or the other way around. It does not help then to point to the intrinsic authority of either tradition, because each of them makes the same claim (which includes the claim to uniqueness—"no other name"). In other words, each tradition asserts that it is founded on a—or, rather, *the*—"Word of God" with which no man may argue. Nor does it help to say that faith is a "leap," because the question now is just *where* one is to leap. There is a road to Mecca as there is a road to Calvary, and the first step on either road (at least for modern man) is in the nature of a "leap of faith." One may surmise that this was never a subjectively real possibility for Barth; others are not so lucky—or, in the perspective of this book, are luckier.

Neo-orthodoxy denies the road and claims the destination as its starting point. Both the denial and the claim must be repudiated. Such repudiation entails a rejection of Barth's counter position of religion and faith (or, more accurately, *Christian* faith). This counter position is spurious. Christianity is one religion among many, and Christian faith ("leaping" or otherwise) is one human possibility among others. To say this is to return to the question that Barth wanted to remove from the agenda: What are the reasons for being a Christian? One asks this question in a particular historical and biographical situation. If that situation is the modern one, the question is beset with all the relativizations of modernity. Neo-orthodoxy seeks to cut through these relativizations in a heroic act of the will and, in consequence, to gain a sort of immunity against the heretical imperative. Heroic the act may well be; it is also illusionary. And so is the immunity to relativization that it purports to produce. The neo-orthodox imagination conjures up characters who confront the "Word of God" in an empirically inaccessible realm. But concrete human beings do not exist in such a realm. Rather, they exist as troubled Swiss pastors, French-speaking Arabs who also want to be Muslims, American college students with access to paperback editions of the Tibetan Book of the Dead, ex-Jews and neo-Hindus, and all the rest of us in the grip of pluralism. *That* is the realm in which religious experience and religious reflection empirically occur. To deny it is to deny the reality of our world. The denial of reality is always a bad place to begin.

Reflecting on Thunder

Now, a very important point must be made in connection with a critique of the neo-orthodox model: The model is of a particular process of *reflection* about religion. It so happens that, as in the case of Barth, the model often denies the notion that its reflection is based on a specific experience. That is, the model tends to be antiempirical, anti-inductive. A critique of the model, of course, need not accept this aspect of it either. Within such a critique, then, it is perfectly logical to ask precisely about the kind of *experience* that underlies the neo-orthodox process of reflection. And the following implication should be noted carefully: A *refusal to follow the neo-orthodox theologian in his process of reflection does not necessarily imply a refusal to take seriously the experience that underlies the reflection.*[28]

Put differently, to reject the neo-orthodox model theoretically is not necessarily to reject its practical (that is, experiential) foundation. Thus an understanding of the empirical foundation of neo-orthodoxy may lead to at least a partial vindication of this approach to religion—*despite* the fact that the neo-orthodox thinker may have denied that such an empirical foundation exists! Put more positively, *within a certain experience neo-orthodoxy does indeed express a valid insight.*

What is this experience?

Mircea Eliade speaks of the "hierophanies," or manifestations of the sacred, which are the great turning points in religious history. These hierophanies are experienced by living human beings, even if some of these experiences are not easily accessible to later generations. One can even put it more sharply: At least in the framework of any this-worldly perspective (of the historian or social scientist as well as of the man-in-the-street), the hierophanies *are* human experiences. Whatever the difficulties of bridging chasms of time and space, every human experience is in principle understandable. Thus a contemporary individual can seek to understand the experiences of the Rig-Veda, of Zoroaster or Isaiah, or of the human beings who built the great temples of the Maya civilization—or, for that matter, the experiences embodied in the religion of so-called primitive cultures. In principle, no human experience is irrevocably alien.

Any hierophany is experienced as the breaking-in of an other reality into the reality of ordinary human life. Needless to stress, the manner of this breaking-in differs greatly between cultures and religious traditions. Thus western Asia (particularly Syria-Palestine, the Arabian peninsula, and Iran) has been characterized by a highly distinctive type of hierophany, the one that has been variously called "kerygmatic" "revelatory," or "prophetic." By contrast, the religious traditions deriving from the subcontinent of India tend to have a very different character —persuasive rather than proclamatory, less dogmatic, less insistent on particular moments of revelation. In either instance, though, the hierophany carries within itself its own warrant of certainty. That is, any individual standing within this experience is compelled by it to exclaim, "Yes, yes, this is truth—and it could be no other." *Every hierophany is like thunder, and the human beings who hear it must feel that this thunder blots out every other sound in the universe.* It could not be otherwise. Speaking in Christian terms, it is perfectly understandable that the community of disciples brought together in Jerusalem and Galilee by the experiences of Calvary, Easter, and Pentecost were compelled to feel, and to say, that "no other name under heaven" but that of Jesus Christ could bring the salvation that had transformed their lives. It could not have been otherwise. The exclusivity intrinsic to any hierophanic experience is further accentuated by the above-mentioned west-Asian context, with its centuries-old tradition of kerygmatic movements and prophetic figures. Islam is probably the most crystalline expression of this kerygmatic-prophetic impulse. While Islam has been somewhat generous in acknowledging prophets before Muhammad (including Abraham, Moses, and Jesus), it was compelled to insist on the exclusive finality of the revelation that came with the Koran: "We revealed the Koran on the Night of Qadr. Would that you knew what the Night of Qadr is like! Better is the Night of Qadr than a thousand months. On that night the angels and the Spirit by their Lord's leave come down with His decrees. That night is peace, till break of day."[29] The "peace" of

which this Koranic passage speaks is precisely the peace of utter
certainty. Yet the day breaks. It even broke for Muhammad.
And that is the point where reflection must set in. To return to
the Christian case, there is no need to invalidate the experience
of the early church in order to question the form in which this
experience was expressed in the preaching and teaching of the
same church. The transformation of experience by reflection is,
of course, a general human phenomenon. Reflection, by its very
nature, always takes place in the cold daylight—on the morning
after, as it were. Reflection about religious experience is no exception to this: Not for those who, in their own lives, experienced the nights of glory in which the sacred manifested itself;
even less for those who, never having lived through such a
night, must make sense of it by way of handed-down accounts
and by analogy with their own, typically feeble, approximations
of the experience.

The accounts of hierophanic experience must be taken with
utmost seriousness as one reflects about them. As will be developed in the next chapter, this precludes the reductionism that
has been so common in modern approaches to religion since
the Enlightenment. But no hierophanic experience must be
taken in isolation, as if there had never been any other. Nor
must the statements of those who have undergone such experience be taken as the only or the authoritative interpretations.
A hierophanic experience, by its very nature, is a state of intoxi-
cation with the divine. In such a state one is prone to say
things that, later on, must be put differently. Al-Ghazali, the
great Muslim thinker who made mysticism acceptable within
Islam, put this very well in discussing some of the more extravagant propositions of the mystics: "They became drunk with a
drunkenness in which their reason collapsed." But then, he
goes on, must come the reflection of soberness: "The words of
lovers when in a state of drunkenness must be hidden away and

not broadcast . . . when their drunkenness abates and the sovereignty of their reason is restored—and reason is God's scale on earth."[80] *Mutatis mutandis*, what al-Ghazali said about the Sufis may also be said about the apostles. And it is hard to think of a more important methodological principle for Christian theological reflection than the insistence that "reason is God's scale on earth!"

But it is time to return once more to the neo-orthodox model. To reiterate, it is a theoretical model, but it too, like all human theorizing, is grounded in experience. This experience can be specified. It is *not* an experience of renewed hierophany; there are indeed such experiences, but the term "neo-orthodoxy" is not appropriate to them. Rather it is an experience of the renewed power of the tradition in which this or that hierophany has been embodied. To distinguish this experience from the cataclysm of original hierophanies is by no means to denigrate it or to overlook its power. The use of Barth as a paradigmatic example should suffice to make this point. Nor does neo-orthodoxy have to take the form of an intellectual movement. It may occur among very unsophisticated people, and even where it finds an intellectual expression, there may be quite nonintellectual people affected by it. The influence of Barthianism in the lives of ordinary Protestants in the Germany of the 1930s is a case in point.

Whatever form neo-orthodoxy takes, it is essentially an experience of returning to the vitality of a tradition—more, a reawakening of that vitality, existentially as much as in reflection. The old words come to live once more. The old power, long-forgotten, manifests itself once more as reality. In this experience, individual lives are dramatically transformed, as are ideas and theories. One of the most dramatic examples of this experience among religious thinkers of the twentieth century is that of Franz Rosenzweig, the German Jewish philosopher who, at one point in his life, was very close to becoming a Christian. Then, on Yom Kippur of 1913, he attended the services in a small Orthodox synagogue in Berlin—and left at the end of the day as a changed man and as a Jew.[31] Rosenzweig was an intellectual of great brilliance and his reconversion experience gave birth to a theoretical opus of impressive scope. But the root experience of such a "return home" to Judaism is common in contemporary America among many people of much more modest intellectual gifts.[32] *Mutatis mutandis,* the same experience has been undergone by Christians and by individuals coming from every other religious background. Those who have this "homecoming" experience invariably feel the need to identify with the community that embodies the tradition they now reaffirm, and because the reconversion is recent and *ipso facto* fragile, this communal identification tends to be very intense.

This is why neo-orthodoxy typically emphasizes strong community ties. Put in sociology-of-religion terms, neo-orthodoxy tends toward sectarianism. In the case of Barth, this came in his turning away from his earlier "existentialistic" individualism to an emphasis on the community of faith; this, of course, is why he called his great systematic opus the *Church Dogmatics.* In the case of reconverts to Judaism, there is the preoccupation with a collective and communal "Jewish identity." This quasi-sectarian thrust of neo-orthodox movements can be explained sociologically. While there are some complex mechanisms involved in this, the root fact is rather simple. Every conversion is fragile; therefore, converts must huddle together for mutual support against an outside world that fails to understand; the sect is the social form par excellence for huddling.[33]

In the neo-orthodox experience—that is, the reconversion experience—the authority of the tradition is regained. It becomes subjectively real to the individual and can then be perceived again as objective reality. This is as true of the man in the street as it is of the theoretician. Both, because of the enormous force of the experience, are impelled to absolutize it. On the level of the man in the street, this impulse expresses itself in an intense commitment to the community. Thus Protestant neo-orthodoxy led to a so-called "rediscovery of the church." On the level of the theoretician, there is the kind of absolutizing that has been analyzed in the Barthian model. On both levels, this creates a fervor and an *élan* that are hard to match.

They are particularly hard to match by any exponents of a liberal approach to religious thought. Inevitably liberals must seem lukewarm and uninspiring when compared with the feisty types that neo-orthodoxy produces. But this is a handicap of any weighing approach in intellectual matters. The individual who proclaims apodictic truth has a psychological advantage over the individual who says, "Now wait a moment, let us look at the other side of this." Trying to get a balanced view is not conducive to a kerygmatic posture. This may be so, but it is also irrelevant as an argument. It would, however, be an error to put the critique of neo-orthodoxy only in terms of a sober and sobering rationality. That would be to repeat the error of the Enlightenment critique of religion. Intellectual rigor is not the only virtue at issue here. There is something else, to which reference was made earlier in connection with the methodological presuppositions of phenomenology: *The determination to remain faithful to one's own experience.*

For many contemporaries there is both the experience of having once been at home in a tradition and that of having left it. Both experiences must be taken seriously, and neither must necessarily be reinterpreted as an aberration. The same applies to the experience of returning home, for those who have had it. It must be *neither* repudiated *nor* absolutized. It is one experience among others, in the individual's own biography and in the larger world of human possibilities. It must be confronted, explored, compared, assessed. If the experience did indeed touch upon something that may be called truth, that truth will reassert itself again and again no matter how many sobering questions are addressed to it. To say this is to reiterate the age-old insight of religious thinkers in all the great traditions: Religious truth has nothing to fear from reason. In this perspective, it should be conceded, "leaps of faith" appear as acts of premature closure—and, perhaps, of a less heroic faith than one first thought. Sometimes it is easier to jump than to hesitate.

4

The Reductive Possibility: Modernizing Tradition

HUMAN BEINGS DO not choose their situation. At best, they may choose how to cope with the situation into which they have been thrown by the accidents of birth and biography. This is as true of the practical as of the cognitive aspects of any situation. An individual does not choose to be male or female, white or black, rich or poor, healthy or sick. To be sure, there are differences in the degree to which individuals may in later life make up for the carelessness with which they selected their parents. Thus some societies make it easier than others for a woman to escape the constraints of her "sex role," or for a member of an oppressed minority to rebel against the oppressing system, or for a poor man to improve his economic status. No doubt there are also differences between individuals as there are differences between societies, and a "strong" individual may overcome sickness or physical handicaps that defeat a "weak" one. All of this, though, does not alter the fundamental fact of the human condition that existential philosophy has aptly termed its "situatedness" or "thrown-ness": Human beings are indeed thrown into a world that is not of their own making. This fundamental fact is the starting point as well as the limitation of any acts of self-assertion, rebellion, or change. The same applies to the cognitive aspects of any situation. An individual does not choose his native language, with all the implications this has for his perceptions of the world and his thinking about the world. Nor does an individual, even if he should be a great philosopher, choose the cognitive milieu within which he must move as an adult, although (if he is very persuasive, or very powerful, or both) he may modify it somewhat before he leaves the scene.

There have been situations in human history in which the gods seemed to be as close as one's fellow men or the natural environment. Perhaps there still are such situations today. The more common situation today, though, is one in which the gods have receded. Sometimes, it appears, they have vanished altogether. This too is a situation that an individual has not chosen. In other words, the world into which human beings are thrown may be full of gods or bereft of them, and either eventuality will determine, at the very least, the starting point for both experience and reflection. The former case may be retrospectively viewed as a lost state of grace or as a happily overcome benightedness, and the latter case may be bemoaned or welcomed. No matter which, it is important that the character of each situation be, first of all, acknowledged. Whatever journey one may wish to undertake, it is necessary to locate the point of departure.

For reasons that have been indicated in earlier chapters, the modern situation has been characterized by a high degree of secularization. Analysts of modernity differ as to how high a degree. It is safe to say, though, that modern consciousness is not conducive to close contact with the gods. This secularity of modern consciousness may, again, be bemoaned or welcomed, depending on one's point of view. In either case it should be acknowledged. It is a given, a datum, of the contemporary situation, especially in Western countries. No one has chosen it. What is open to a considerable degree of choice, however, is one's response to this situation. And an understanding of various options for this response is, of course, the main topic of this book.

The orthodox mind is the one that has not as yet perceived the character of the modern situation (or perhaps it would be more accurate to say that the orthodox mind is not, in actual fact, within that situation). The neo-orthodox mind, by an act of will, denies the modern situation at least to the extent of denying the import of its cognitive challenges. Put differently, for the orthodox nothing has happened yet; the neo-orthodox acts *as if* nothing had happened. Put differently again, the orthodox continues to affirm the tradition "innocently"; the neo-orthodox has lost this "innocence" and is compelled to reaffirm the tradition in an often mind-wrenching effort. At the opposite pole of a spectrum of possible responses is a mind that perceives the tradition as no longer affirmable except by way of a comprehensive translation into the categories of modern consciousness. Here the perception is the precise opposite of the orthodox or neo-orthodox one: *Everything* has happened.

The most radical form of this perception has been the classical statement by Nietzsche that God has died. In the 1960s, in connection with what was then known as the "death of God movement" in American Protestant theology, it was restated by Thomas Altizer as follows: "A theology that chooses to meet our time, a theology that accepts the destiny of history, must first assess the theological significance of the death of God. We must realize that the death of God is an historical event, that God has died in our cosmos, in our history, in our *Existenz*."[1] Now, the interesting thing here is that Altizer perceived the death of God as a starting point for an enterprise of *Christian theology*. By contrast, of course, most others (emphatically including Nietzsche) who concluded that God had died assumed *ipso facto* that further theologizing made as little sense as further affirmations of Christian faith. Altizer and his associates, on the other hand, wanted to continue both believing and reflecting, as Christians, by means of categories that (or so they maintained) had *not* died. Clearly, the self-designation of this reinterpretation as "radical" is convincing. Its details will not be pursued here, but it is useful to recall it to show the extreme forms possible in the wake of the perception that the modern situation has changed everything for religious experience and religious thought.

Bargaining with Modernity

Once again, the perspective of the sociology of knowledge is useful in grasping the dynamics of the reductive possibility. For this possibility, no more and no less than any of the other options in the contemporary situation, does not occur in some sort of Platonic heaven or theoretical sphere isolated from the realities of ordinary life. It is based on experience, pretheoretical experience, and it has specific plausibility structures that can be analyzed sociologically. Specifically, the experience here is of a modern consciousness in which religious traditions, including one's own, have become dim, and this consciousness in turn has a social context. In principle, this experience of the secularizing force of modernity is shared by intellectuals and nonintellectuals. The sociology of religion has demonstrated how very ordinary people, who rarely read books and never write them, have been affected by it. One may mention here, for example, the pioneering work of Gabriel LeBras, the French sociologist who began to study the impact of urban life on religion in the 1930s. Thus LeBras studied what happened to the religious life of Bretons who migrated to Paris. At that time (and this may well be so even today) Brittany was one of the most strongly Catholic areas of France and Bretons scored highest on any indicator of religious commitment. All this changed drastically and suddenly as soon as Breton migrants arrived in Paris, to the point that LeBras remarked that there must be a magical piece of pavement in the Gare du Nord (the railroad station where most Bretons arrived in the capital) which changed good Catholics into agnostics or at least non-practitioners. In actual fact, of course, no magic is in play in this kind of transformation (as LeBras knew well). The sociologist of knowledge can describe what happens in such cases by saying that the plausibility structure of traditional belief and practice is severely weakened by the migration, and once this is understood, there is nothing mysterious about the changed relationship to the religious tradition. Indeed, in this perspective it would be a mystery if that relationship did *not* change. But working-class migrants do not write books or spin out theories (or, probably more accurately, such theories as they spin out remain unrecorded). It is all the more important to understand that, at bottom, the intellectual (here, the theologian) who does theorize and who records his theorizing in books is subject to the very same dynamics of plausibility and implausibility.

The modern situation, then, brings about an adversary relationship between a socially dominant secularity and the religious consciousness. Put differently, the dominant secularity exerts *cognitive pressure* upon the religious consciousness. The adjective should be stressed in the italicized phrase. For it is not necessarily a matter of overt social processes—say, of disapproval, ridicule, let alone persecution. Much more importantly, it is a matter of a gap between the cognitive presuppositions of the religious consciousness and the cognitive presuppositions of

the surrounding social milieu. To the extent that the latter is
more powerful (as the glittering world of Parisian metro-
politanism is more powerful than the low-status subculture of
Breton migrants), the cognitive pressures emanate from it.
Some people, intellectuals as well as others, resolve this problem by giving in to the pressures. This means, quite simply,
that they give up the cognitively deviant beliefs and practices
of their religious background. They may do this loudly and
explicitly, informing everyone that they are no longer Catholics
(or whatever they were originally). More likely, their secularization will be unobtrusive and implicit. In either case, they no
longer have this particular problem.

Other people, however, are not willing to give up their tradition so readily. Whether it is simply because of habit or senti-
mental attachment, or whether it is because they want to
remain faithful to what for them has been an experience of
truth, they seek to salvage at least the core of the tradition in
the changed situation. On various levels of sophistication, from
the level of theological seminars to that of conversations in a
factory lunchroom, what happens then is a process of *cognitive
bargaining*. Just because the pressures of secularity are so
strong, not everything can be salvaged once this process begins.
(Let it be recalled here that the neo-orthodox option is precisely the refusal to enter the bargaining process in the first
place!) Thus there will be compromises. Certain outward
manifestations of piety may be surrendered, in the hope that
an irreducible core can be held on to. On the cognitive level,
some traditional propositions will be abandoned, others ad-
hered to. For example, Jesus' miracle of the loaves and fishes
will be given up (or explained in naturalistic terms, which
amounts to the same thing)—but not the miracle of the resurrection. Or it will be conceded that Paul was quite wrong in his
views on women or on slavery—but not on the justification of
sinners. And so on and so forth. (It will be remarked already

that there is a built-in problem in this bargaining process—namely, that secularity, like all dominant worldviews, is very hungry, so that it is difficult to call a halt to the giveaways.)

The history of Protestant theology since Schleiermacher can quite adequately be described as a great drama of cognitive bargaining. And, of course, it was Protestant theological liberalism that did the most intensive bargaining. An unsympathetic observer might also call it a strategy of orderly retreat. Enough has been said already to indicate that lack of sympathy for the liberal enterprise in theology is not at issue in this book, whatever may be its other failings. This means, to put it bluntly, that some measure of cognitive bargaining with modern consciousness is deemed to be inevitable here. This means further, however, that it is sometimes difficult to draw a sharp line between compromise and surrender. One man's reductionism may be another's reasonable accommodation. Still, a line *can* be drawn—to wit, at the point where modern consciousness becomes the ultimate criterion of all religious affirmations. Put differently, it is possible to speak of reduction when the basic method of religious thought consists in abandoning all elements of the tradition that are deemed to be incompatible with the cognitive assumptions of modernity. There are different ways in which this has been done. Once more, as was attempted in the preceding chapter for the option of restored deduction, the procedure followed here will be to look at one important case in the recent history of Protestant theology and then to ask to what extent this case represents a broader cognitive model or strategy.

Bargaining Away "Mythology"

The case to be looked at is the program of so-called "demythologization" proposed by the German Protestant theolo-

gian Rudolf Bultmann during World War II and violently
argued over for at least the following decade.[2] Bultmann originally proposed his program in an essay that could not be published at the time, during the last years of the war, when the
Nazis had virtually stopped all theological publishing. The
essay, entitled "New Testament and Mythology," circulated
within a quite small circle of theologians in mimeographed
form and only emerged from this subterranean existence after
the end of the war.[3] It then created a storm of controversy almost immediately, first in the German-speaking milieu and
then internationally. Exciting though the essay was in itself, its
impact was undoubtedly augmented by the stature of its author. Bultmann had established his reputation as a New Testament scholar as early as the 1920s and many thought of him as
the foremost representative of this field in at least a generation.
He had been close to the "dialectical theology" movement, had
been all his life not only a university professor (mostly at Marburg) but also an actively committed Lutheran churchman,
and had belonged to the so-called Confessing Church in its resistance to Nazism. The radicality of his proposals, which
seemed to many a strange resurgence of a theological liberalism
deemed to have been buried for good by Karl Barth, thus had
the shock value of a total surprise. Indeed, it had some of the
character of a theological man-bites-dog story. Bultmann himself made his observations with a great sense of urgency, feeling
that something along the lines of his program was necessary if
the Protestant church was to survive in the postwar period.

Bultmann's program of demythologization is based on a
specific understanding both of mythology and of the mythological character of the New Testament. Mythology is understood by Bultmann as a pattern of thought in which the otherworldly is represented as acting within the world, or, put
differently, in which the empirical world is ongoingly penetrated by forces from beyond it. Not only do these supernatural

forces break into and interfere with events in nature, but the human personality itself is open to constant influence from another world—by gods and demons, miracle and magic—in an extreme form in the belief that human individuals can be possessed by either sacred or satanic spirits (as, respectively, in the early Christian experience of possession by the Holy Spirit at Pentecost or in the various accounts of exorcisms conducted by Jesus and the apostles). All of this is based on a cosmology in which the world of human life is part and parcel of an order that contains both the natural and the supernatural. In the Bible this is what Bultmann calls the "three-story universe," the earth being the middle ground on which beings from "up above" (the heavens, from which, among others, Christ descended in the incarnation and to which he returned in his ascension) and from "down below" (the underworld, the realm of the dead and of the powers of hell) engage in cosmic struggles. This entire mythological view of reality is in sharp conflict with the modern view, which has been shaped by science and which understands the cosmos as a closed system of empirical causalities. The mythological worldview also contradicts the modern view of the human personality, which, whatever its relation to the causalities of nature, is also deemed to be closed to alien forces acting upon it (let alone penetrating it) from a world beyond.

The mythological worldview permeates every part of the New Testament—the Gospels, the Pauline epistles, the entire scope of the Christian kerygma. In this assertion, of course, Bultmann could utilize his vast command of historical-critical scholarship, which had borne fruit in a long list of publications. Thus Bultmann saying that the worldview of the New Testament was mythological carried a very different weight from the same statement being made by this or that rationalist critic of Christianity. No one could argue that Bultmann did not know

whereof he spoke! But he said more than that. He insisted that
the mythological character of the New Testament lies not only
in certain cosmological assumptions that could be put aside as
irrelevant to the gospel message, as had been the practice of
classical theological liberalism. The very content of the Christian message of salvation, the kerygma itself, is couched in
mythological language. It presupposes a long list of undoubtedly mythological conceptions of reality: The pre-existence of
Christ in heaven; his incarnation as a human being; his
crucifixion as offering atonement on behalf of sinners; his resurrection as the victory in a cosmic battle; salvation through
Christ as the removal of the curse of sin inflicted upon humanity by Adam; Christ's ascension to heaven and enthronement
on the right hand of God; his return on the clouds at the end
of history; the resurrection and judgment of the dead; the presence of the risen Christ in the church through the Holy Spirit
and the sacraments. All these are mythological concepts,
mythological thought patterns, part and parcel of a mythological view of the cosmos. And as such they constitute a view
of the world which modern man is incapable not only of accepting but even of grasping. They are, in Bultmann's words,
"finished" (*erledigt*). If Christianity depends upon them for
its continuing existence, then Christianity itself is "finished."

If Bultmann's program depends on a specific understanding
of mythology and of the mythological character of the New
Testament, it depends equally on a specific understanding of
modern man and his cognitive capabilities. Although Bultmann devotes remarkably little space in his original essay to an
exposition of this understanding of modern man, it is central to
his position. Not surprisingly, it became one of the important
foci of the later controversy. Be this as it may, modern man, for
Bultmann, is above all defined negatively: He is one who must
not be expected to believe in all this mythology.

Man is not capable of freely choosing his view of the world, which rather is given to him by his historical situation. Modern man, even if he wanted to think in mythological terms, is bound to the view of the world which science has given him. He may try to convince himself that he can indeed accept the mythology of the New Testament, but this is an exercise in self-delusion. There have indeed been efforts in modern times to resurrect mythological thinking, as in the Nazis' "myth of the twentieth century" or various occultist movements. But it is interesting that even these remythologizations have pretended to be based on "scientific" insights. This incapability of modern man to think mythologically is summed up in what is probably the most often quoted sentence in Bultmann's essay: "One cannot use electric light and radio, call upon modern medicine in case of illness, and at the same time believe in the world of spirits and miracles of the New Testament."[4] It is worth dwelling for a moment on the opening phrase of this sentence, "one cannot"—in German, *man kann nicht.*" In its lapidary character it recalls the classical statement of Luther's, "Here I stand, I can do no other" (*"Ich kann nicht anders"*). There is here the same undertone of relentless honesty, of relying courageously on the insights of one's own conscience. But now (and what a change!) the *content* of this stance has shifted from the biblical tradition to the alleged worldview of modern man. The pathos of this shift is only underlined by the obvious fact that Bultmann did not intend it.

What follows from all this is that, if Christianity is to be meaningful to modern man, it must be demythologized radically, at its heart as well as on its fringes. One cannot give in a little here, a little there—in the terms used earlier in this chapter, one cannot engage in cognitive bargaining. Rather, one must reject or accept the mythological worldview as a whole.

Once this is understood, there is really no honest choice. The question then becomes not *whether* the Christian message is to be demythologized but *how* this is to be done. At this point Bultmann very clearly sets himself off from older liberal attempts that could also be designated as demythologization programs. Classical liberalism demythologized the New Testament by translating it either into ethics or into some type of mystical experience. Thus what Christianity is supposed to be "really" all about is the ethics of Jesus or, alternatively, an experience of communion with God of which Jesus or the early Christians may serve as exemplars. Here Bultmann can speak with the full authority of the New Testament scholar: Christianity, as proclaimed by the New Testament, is *neither* a system of ethics *nor* a mystical discipline. To maintain either would be to abandon the kerygma along with the mythology, and this would be the real end of Christianity. The kerygma must be maintained, but it must be communicated to modern man in a nonmythological form.

This form, for Bultmann, is *existential* and to expound it he utilizes the conceptual apparatus of existential philosophy (especially Martin Heidegger's). Bultmann is sensitive to the charge that he might be retrojecting into the New Testament an understanding of human life first thought up by modern existentialism. This is not what he is doing, he insists. The modern philosophical categories simply serve to illuminate the human condition as such, and their usefulness for the theologian should be welcomed. What is more, the New Testament itself calls for its demythologization, for only thus can one reconcile its inner contradictions. For instance, the New Testament on the one hand sees man as fallen under bondage to demonic forces and on the other hand calls man to decision. One demythologizes the New Testament, and *ipso facto* resolves its contradictions, by uncovering the underlying existential concern—which, in this instance, is the understanding that man cannot free himself of his own accord from the anguish of his condition but must rely on God's action to do so. The kerygma addresses itself precisely to this existential predicament, today as in New Testament times, and Heidegger's philosophical categories simply serve to make this understandable.

The problems of the historian with the New Testament are solved in an elegant (critics would certainly say, an overly elegant) way. The New Testament is concerned not with abstract and impersonal history of events in the past (the events of the historical Jesus) but with the significance of these events for the individual's own existence. In other words, the New Testament is not interested in historiography but in the history of the risen Christ in the existence of those who believe in him.[5] Thus the Easter faith of the Christian becomes sovereignly independent of whatever empirical facts may or may not underlie the myth of the empty tomb. In other words, the New Testament is interpreted as offering a certain view of human existence in the world. It is a rather dismal view, which makes the correlation with the gloomy categories of modern existentialism credible. In this world man exists in impermanence and in the face of death (Heidegger called this "living toward death"). Therefore, human existence is marked by permanent anxiety (Kierkegaard's *Angst*, Heidegger's *Sorge*). Man is lost in this world of anxiety, in bondage, in need of being freed. His efforts to free himself are doomed to failure (the plays of Jean-Paul Sartre are probably the most eloquent expression of this assessment of all man's efforts to find an "exit"—there is none, Sartre insists). This failure is rooted in the very nature of man, in what Luther called the human "heart bent back upon itself" (*cor incurvatus in se ipsum*). Life in the spirit and in faith is the experience of liberation coming from the outside, through Christ. Faith in the kerygma frees man from bondage and

opens him up toward God and the world. The same faith reduces the anguish of this world to insignificance, wipes away
the burden of the past, and allows man to become free for a future that is open-ended. But this experience is not mystical, not
even psychological. It is always the result of an act, a decision
(here, once again, Kierkegaard's "leap of faith" puts in an appearance). At the same time, this act/decision is apprehended
by the believer as a free gift of God's grace, never to be safely
possessed or to be verified logically or empirically.

All these existential propositions (so Bultmann argues) do
not hinge upon a mythological worldview. On the contrary,
they are profoundly and urgently relevant for modern man in
his specific historical situation. The Christian life is not to be
understood as relating to supernatural processes or events, past
or present. It is entirely located within this world. It can never
be verified in terms of the miraculous, can never be taken out
of the natural context of human existence. To try and do otherwise is to reiterate the option rejected by Jesus when Satan
urged him to jump off the pinnacle of the Temple in order to
prove his Messiahship. Although Bultmann does not use this
term in his original essay, it is fair to say that demythologization implies secularization.

Bultmann was very much troubled by the question of
whether this understanding of human existence was possible
without Christ, Christian faith, or Christian kerygma. He conceded that modern existentialism showed that at least the anthropological presuppositions of this understanding were possible for the non-Christian. But he pointed out that modern
existentialism would not have appeared in history (in the history of *Western* thought) without the New Testament,
Luther, Kierkegaard, and Dostoyevsky. Apart from that,
though, Christianity maintains over against existentialism that
an understanding of the human condition as *Angst*, lostness,

and so forth is not enough. Man cannot free himself from this condition. He can be freed only by an act of the transcendent God. The line between a Christian-existential and a secular-existential anthropology seems perilously thin here, and Bultmann was very much aware of this. He was further aware of the objection (made much of by his critics later on) that speaking of a transcendent God acting in the world may, by his own definition, be called mythological language. The point remains unresolved, but Bultmann reiterates that it can be resolved in the act of faith itself; the Barthian flavor of this position is not accidental.

This act of God in Christ is itself demythologized. In essence, the act is understood as taking place here and now, in the meeting between kerygma and faith. The Easter faith in the resurrection is no longer faith in a historical event some two thousand years ago, fixated in the myth of an empty tomb and of ghostlike apparitions of the crucified Jesus, but rather it is faith in the God who meets the contemporary individual as the Christian message is proclaimed to him. This is eloquently summed up in this sentence: "Christ, the crucified and risen, meets us in the World of proclamation, nowhere else. Just the faith in this Word is in truth the Easter faith."[6] There is here a classically Protestant view of the immense importance of preaching, and it should be remarked in passing that Bultmann was all his life a preacher, and apparently a very good one.[7] Eschatology too is demythologized from a cosmic to an existential frame of reference. It is no longer, finally, some obscure and historically unreconstructable events in Palestine that matter but what occurs every Sunday in this or that church in Germany in the mid-twentieth century. Cross and resurrection are no longer cosmic events in a mythological universe but events brought about by God in the existence of contemporary individuals.

If demythologization frees the individual Christian from having to engage in mental acrobatics upon reading the Bible, it also has a liberating effect on Christian theology. No longer must the theologian be in a constantly defensive position before each advance of biblical scholarship or modern science. The Christian message is transposed onto a plane where these can no longer touch it. One could imagine an extreme case. Suppose a set of motion-picture cameras had been (somewhat precociously) trained on the burial place of Jesus on Easter morning. Suppose that the film were discovered by an archaeologist, and that it showed nothing at all, or perhaps some of the disciples rolling away the stone and taking off with the body under cover of darkness. All this would yet leave intact Bultmann's Easter faith and, presumably, God's act in that faith. Thus, curiously (or perhaps not so curiously), Bultmann's notion of faith ends up in an empirically nonfalsifiable stance very similar to Barth's.

A Translation Model

Bultmann's proposal to demythologize the New Testament and the Christian message as a whole is the work of a bold thinker of great scholarship and sophistication. Whatever one may think of the merits of the proposal, one must admire it both on the level of its intellectual force and of its author's personal integrity. It is nevertheless important to see that it does not stand by itself as an attempt to deal with the cognitive discontents of modernity. It is one of a genre. Indeed, Bultmann's procedure may be looked upon as a model for a specific type of cognitive strategy. To see it in this way, of course, one must abstract the essential structure of the argument from the contents of the particular case. As one does this the model emerges as a possibility not only for Christian theologians but for any other religious tradition.

The model always begins by what purports to be a sure analysis of the modern situation, or more accurately, of the consciousness of modern man. This consciousness, supposedly, is secularized and *ipso facto* incapable of assenting to the traditional definitions of reality. That much, of course, could also be maintained by an orthodox or neo-orthodox thinker, who would then, however, go on something like this: "Yes, this is how modern man is. How deplorable! And how totally wrong! Let us now go about the task of converting him." But this is precisely what the model at issue does *not* do. It jumps from the empirical diagnosis that modern consciousness is indeed secularized to the epistemological assumption that this secularity is superior to whatever worldviews (mythological or what-have-you) preceded it. Perhaps this is the true "leap" of this model! Sometimes this passage from empirical diagnosis to epistemology is clearly indicated. This happens when *reasons* are given as to why modern man is right on so many points where his ancestors were wrong. Depending on the philosophical standpoint of the one working this model, these reasons will naturally differ, but they will always have to include the assumption that human beings in the recent past have discovered methods of knowing the truth that were previously unknown or imperfect. In other words, there is an assumption here of a cognitively superior status of modern man. Interestingly, though, quite often no reasons are given at all for this assumption. This is very much so in Bultmann's case. The cognitive superiority of all those electricity- and radio-users over the authors of the New Testament is apodictically stated as a self-evident fact. It seems not to have occurred to Bultmann that, in certain respects, modern man may be cognitively *inferior* to human beings in earlier periods of history. More of this shortly.

Within the model it is also quite clear just which aspects of the religious tradition are no longer assertable in the face of modern consciousness. These aspects may be differently described—as mythological, supernaturalistic, otherworldly and so on. But what is intended here is always that view of reality with which Bultmann identified mythology: The view that the empirical world of men is penetrated, or at least penetrable, by forces and beings from another world. Secularity, against this, asserts the closed character of the universe—there are no miracles, no demons, no supernatural realms of any sort. Insofar as the model still wants to hold on to an alleged core of the religious tradition (which, in a Christian case, minimally means some notion of God as well as of the redemptive significance of Christ), that core must then be articulable in terms that exclude the "no longer possible" definitions of reality. In other words, the tradition must be demythologized, stripped of its supernaturalistic trappings—indeed, it must be cognitively secularized.

For this reason, at the heart of the model is a *translation procedure*. The basic rule for this is simple: Terms of transcendent reference in the tradition must be either eliminated (in the case of those deemed marginal) or translated into terms of immanent reference (in the case of those deemed part of the core to be preserved). Put differently, references to *other* worlds are translated into terms referring to *this* world, the superempirical is translated into the empirical, the more-than-human into the human. Such translation, it is argued, will make the tradition once more acceptable to modern man, because it will no longer require of him that he give up his (supposedly superior) worldview. But it would be unfair to leave the impression that the motive of those who employ this model is simply tactical, in the sense of "What can we say to keep people in our churches?" Much more basic is the cognitive force of modern secularity and the pressure it exerts on the mind of religious thinkers. In other words, never mind what happens to all those other people, the finally pressing question for the religious thinker is "How can I stay in the church—and continue to think honestly?" This assumes, of course, that a particular thinker *wants* to stay in the church (or synagogue, or Muslim community). But then, if he did not want this, he would have no need for this model of theorizing about religion!

There must, then, be some sort of translation. There will be great differences in the languages employed by the translators. In principle, any language will do—provided it meets the criterion of being secular in its content and secularizing in its effect on the tradition. As has been shown, Bultmann employed the language of existential philosophy for his attempt at translation. But there is no compelling necessity why this philosophy rather than another should be used, or why the language must be philosophical at all.[8]

It would be a worthwhile enterprise to compose a "comparative grammar," so to speak, of the various languages that have been used to secularize religious thought and thereby to reduce it to categories of a purported modern consciousness. This book is not the place for such an enterprise. But it may be useful to indicate in very broad outline what the typical possibilities have been.

The possibility that Bultmann rejected, that of portions of classical Protestant liberalism, is the translation of the religious tradition into terms of ethics. In a Christian milieu this will typically mean an interpretation of Jesus as a great ethical teacher or moral exemplar, but it is important to stress that Christians are not the only ones who can perform such a translation. *Mutatis mutandis*, Jews, Muslims, Buddhists, and others can do the same. Nor has the critique of Christian theological liberalism in this respect, a critique that clearly demonstrated the misinterpretation of the New Testament involved in this translation into ethics, ended this possibility within the Christian sphere either. Thus it is quite possible to concede that Jesus himself or the early Christians were not primarily interested in ethical questions, and yet to go on to argue that *for modern man* that *is* the major interest. In other words, even if Jesus did not think of himself as a teacher of morality, we are free to take him as such. It is also relevant to point out that, quite apart from theologians, ordinary people in many countries think of their religious traditions in precisely these terms. Thus many Christians and Jews in contemporary America will say that they have little use for the properly religious contents of their respective traditions, but that they greatly value the ethical teachings—which is why they send their children to be instructed in churches and synagogues!

The translation of a religious tradition into terms of ethics satisfies the above-stated criterion very neatly. Ethics can, indeed must, be stated in secular terms—that is, in terms that refer to the empirical world in which human beings relate to each other. To strive for justice, to be compassionate, to have a concern for the poor or oppressed—or more specific ethical concerns, ranging from sexual codes to the abolition of violence —all these need not have anything to do with any supernatural definitions of reality. If it can be maintained that what Christianity (or Judaism, or Islam, and so on) "is really all about" is a certain attitude with regard to these moral problems, then the translation into secularity has been accomplished. Needless to say, very divergent ethical contents can be used to "fill" this model. Thus the alleged moral teachings of Christianity may be abstinence from extramarital sex or universal tolerance for all expressions of sexuality, total pacificism or self-sacrifice in

just wars, racial tolerance or a belief in the "white man's burden," and so on almost ad infinitum. The important thing is
that one can maintain any of these moral positions and justify
them by an ethical theory without getting embroiled in "mythology."

A different language is provided by psychology. What the
religious tradition "is really all about" here is not ethics but the
mental health or wholeness of the individual. In some respects
this variant of the model is similar to those versions that employ the languages of modern philosophy. And, of course, there
are as many subvarieties of this as there are different forms of
modern psychology and psychotherapy. As in all these translations, the procedure can be very sophisticated or very crude intellectually. The translation of religion into psychological language has been very popular in America, possibly reaching its
heyday to date in the 1950s with such prophets of psychoreli-
gious salvation as Norman Vincent Peale. This continues
today, ranging from the complexities of the Jungians or the followers of Abraham Maslow to the latest products of the pop-
therapy industry. The basic cognitive strategy remains the
same, regardless of the differences in psychological theory and
therapeutic practice.

Currently in vogue is the employment of political language
in the translation of religious traditions into secular terms. This
type of translation is, of course very close to the ethical one,
except for its stress on collective problems and on activism. At
the moment the prevailing form of this is ideologically "on the
left"—it tends to be Marxist in theoretical inspiration, is an-
ticapitalist and anti-"bourgeois" in attitude, and expresses itself
in political programs seeking to promote this or that vision of
socialism. It is all the more important to perceive that there is
nothing necessary to this particular ideological coloration. Precisely the same cognitive procedure can have a right-wing char-

acter, and often enough has had just that. Thus there is a long
history in America of people identifying Christianity with the
American "way of life," with liberal democracy, and indeed
with capitalism. It is quite possible, given the vacillations of
politics, that this older version of politicoreligious ideology will
come to the fore again. After all, Jesus as a premature Che
Guevara is no more plausible intrinsically than Jesus as the prototype of the successful salesman (as he was represented in
that notorious bestseller of the 1920s, *The Man Nobody
Knows*). And in Latin America today, for every young priest
who believes that *the* task of Christians is to build socialism
there is a young army officer who thinks that what Christianity
"is really all about" is the fight against Communism and mini-
skirts.

Quite apart from the question of whether this model is correct in its perception of modern man and his consciousness, it
has a built-in difficulty that has already been mentioned: It is
difficult to stop the secularization process and, after a certain
point, it becomes self-liquidating. On the theoretical level, one
of Bultmann's key difficulties illustrates the problem very
clearly: Why omit the action of God in Christ (or, for that
matter, the very notion of God acting) from the demythologization program? And, if one includes this too in the program,
what is left of Christianity to be salvaged? On the practical
level, the problem is really quite simple: All the secular benefits
that the tradition is now supposed to "really be about" can be
had without the tradition. After all, one can be a good person
morally without identifying oneself as a Christian or a Jew, and
psychotherapy and politics similarly do not require religious labels anymore in much of the world. So why bother with the old
labels? Sociologically this suggests the hypothesis that people
who do bother do so because of a lingering attachment to the

tradition that is likely to be transitory, and some data of the sociology of religion (at least in this country) seem to bear out this hypothesis.

Critique of the Model

The difficulty of the reductive option that can be summed up in the proposition that this option tends to be self-liquidating is, essentially, a sociological one and, as such, is not a sufficient critique. After all, one might be convinced that to translate a religious tradition into secular terms will indeed tend to make that tradition obsolete—and nevertheless proceed to do just this, not because one believes this to be a good survival strategy but because one believes it to be true. But that is not the only ground for criticism. There are more substantive objections to be made. These were made at great length against Bultmann's demythologization program; *mutatis mutandis*, they also apply to the general translation model, as it has been called here. It is the latter application, of course, rather than the details of the controversy over Bultmann, which is the present concern.

Bultmann was sharply criticized for his concept of myth. This was done both by critics from the theological right, who felt that Bultmann had gone too far, and critics from the left, who felt that he had not gone far enough.[9] One of the most comprehensive critiques of this came, very interestingly, from outside theology—from the philosopher Karl Jaspers, who argued that mythological language was necessary, in modern times as in any previous period of history, if man is to come to terms with the transcendent dimensions of his existence. It follows that any program to demythologize a religious tradition will result, willy-nilly, in a fundamental impoverishment of

thought—to wit, the impoverishment of the loss of transcendence.[10] Jaspers was not particularly interested in the defense of
the Christian tradition; those who were made the point over
and over again that, by Bultmann's own definition of mythology, it makes no sense to demythologize the New Testament
but then stop short of demythologizing the act of God in
Christ—that too would have to be called a myth, and after
that myth is gotten rid of along with all the other myths, nothing is left of the Christian kerygma except a bit of existentialist
anthropology.

It is not accidental that Bultmann's definition of *mythology*
strongly resembles the definition of *religion* developed in chapter 2 of this book. The core experience in all human religion, it
was argued there, is precisely one of interpenetration, of an
other reality invading or impinging upon the reality of ordinary
human life. Needless to say, this interpenetration of worlds
need not take any particular form such as the cosmologies of
Judaism or Hellenism in the background of the New Testament authors. But to deny the validity of *any* view of the world
in terms of such interpenetration is *ipso facto* to invalidate all
religious experience as such. Modern secular thought has, of
course, done just that. Modern secularity does indeed supply a
cosmos in which there is no supernatural, no world beyond, no
visitations from such a world. But if one gives credence to this
cosmos, one ought to draw the proper consequences, as has
been done by a long line of secular thinkers since the Enlightenment. One of the proper consequences is to give up the use
of metaphors deriving from a very different cosmos. In other
words, if the worldview of modern secularity is true, one should
have the decency to stop using religious language. The historical fact that this or that modern philosophy, moral insight, psy-
chotherapeutic technique or political agenda has Christian *origins* is not enough of a motive to go on calling oneself a

Christian. Historical gratitude, as it were, is not a motive for faith.

Bultmann was also severely taken to task for his understanding of modern man and modern consciousness. From the theological right, of course, that criticism implied a charge of idolatry. As was to be expected, that charge was made by Karl Barth with customary vehemence.[11] But Bultmann's absolutization of a modern worldview can also be criticized from positions that are very far from neo-orthodoxy. Thus Jaspers criticized Bultmann for a wrong conception of modern science and its relation to philosophy; Bultmann's presuppositions, Jaspers charged, were not those of science but of a rather crude "scientism," which belonged to the nineteenth rather than the twentieth century. Furthermore, modern man was not at all the flat, positivistic creature that Bultmann would have one believe.

The lack of critical distance in regard to modern consciousness is not just a failing of Bultmann's. It is common to all versions of the translation model. All share the conviction (sometimes explicit, more often implied) that modern man stands on some sort of cognitive pinnacle, from which he can survey and overcome the shortcomings of all his predecessors. This conviction, upon closer scrutiny, is very hard to sustain. Thus one may agree that the dominance of modern technology (Bultmann's electricity, radio, and medicine) has indeed affected the worldview of modern man. One may even agree that, in some areas, there have been cognitive gains in this. But has this really been so in *all* areas? Is it not possible that, while modern man has gained some valid insights into reality, he has also *lost* some equally valid insights? And, among these is there not to be placed high on the list modern man's weakened relation to the realm of transcendence? Even if it is conceded (which ought not to be conceded) that, the moment one starts using an electric toothbrush or watching the CBS news, the world of the gods recedes into implausibility, is this necessarily an advance over the author of the Gospel of John (not to mention Socrates, Aeschylus, and the Buddha)? To ask these questions is to begin answering them. The answers are not supportive of Bultmann's presuppositions nor of the presuppositions of any other form of secularizing theology.

In actual fact, modern consciousness is a far more complicated phenomenon. It does indeed contain a secularizing component, as has been indicated in this book before, but the reasons for this can be analyzed sociologically and have little if anything to do with some sort of epistemological superiority of modern man. A grasp of the sociological determinants of modern consciousness (including the key determinant of pluralism) makes it difficult either to absolutize or to radically denigrate that consciousness. History brings forth and dissolves one structure of consciousness after another. Each one is to be taken seriously and looked at in terms of its possible insights. In this respect, modern consciousness is one among many historically available structures—no more, no less. To see the matter in this way precludes any apodictic statements as to what modern men "can no longer" believe. In this as in many other matters, historical understanding and the sociology of knowledge conspire to produce a healthy skepticism about the taken-for-granted certainties of any age, one's own included.

Finally, Bultmann has been criticized (again most comprehensively by Jaspers) for a very one-sided view of the human condition, a very pessimistic one. In his case, the gloomy categories of Heideggerian existentialism served to explicate that view. But is the human condition really as bad as all that? Quite a few people, including quite a few philosophers, would deny it. Furthermore, the plausibility of a worldview based on *Angst* and the like may be understood in sociology-of-

knowledge terms (a point made in the preceding chapter in
discussing neo-orthodoxy). Other versions of the translation
model, of course, use other categories. But it is interesting that
many of them share an overall pessimistic bias: Things are very
bad indeed—and *therefore* a particular set of salvific symbols is
plausible. This pessimistic bias is prominent in both the psy-
chotherapeutic and the political versions of the model that are
current today. Human beings are beset with all these crippling
neuroses—and therefore desperately in need of therapy. Or
they are oppressed and alienated by a particular socioeconomic
system—and therefore call out for revolutionary redemption.
Now it so happens that a lot of people feel neither psycho-
logically crippled nor socially oppressed. The typical way of
handling this inconvenient fact is to use it to show *just how
bad* things actually are: Things are *so* bad that people don't
even know that they are crippled, crazy, exploited and so on!
The Freudian theory of repression and the Marxist theory of
false consciousness are tailored to perform this trick of turning
around all contrary evidence. But that is another story. Suffice
it to say here that the plausibility of many versions of the translation model collapses if one has more optimistic notions of
human life.

Man as Symbolizer and as Symbol

Ludwig Feuerbach's concept of projection was not the earliest but the classical formulation of the basic translation procedure. Feuerbach understood religion as a gigantic projection
of human concerns onto the cosmos: What religion is "really
all about" is human life, human reality, human fears and
hopes. Consequently Feuerbach's program was the translation
of theology into anthropology: Propositions that refer to super-

human realities are to be reduced to propositions with a solely human reference. This was indeed a Copernican revolution in man's reflection about religion, and it has had vast consequences in the history of ideas. Most immediately, it was the basis of Marx's reinterpretation of the human condition (as he put it, everyone must pass through the "fiery brook" of this cognitive revolution before being able to understand anything at all about man, history, or society). But it vitally shaped both Freud and Nietzsche, and it hovers over every other program of secularizing the religious view of reality (including the programs of thinkers who are unaware of Feuerbach). It is, as it were, the *Ur*-form or clue-concept of all reductionism.

Nor can Feuerbach be dismissed easily. The historical, social, and psychological sciences of the last two centuries have indeed demonstrated beyond the shadow of a doubt that every religious tradition is full of projections of a variety of very thisworldly human interests. Thus every strand of the New Testament literature has what biblical scholars have called its *Sitz im Leben*—that is, its sociohistorical "location." Thus a religious tradition can indeed be located in terms of economic circumstances (Marx), emotional frustrations (Freud), or collective resentments (Nietzsche). The modern scientific study of religion would not be possible without these demonstrations of mundane determinants of what purports to be extramundane. Let it be stipulated in principle (one may, of course, quarrel with specific interpretations) that these demonstrations are valid. The point is, quite simply, that this is not the whole story. An analogy may be helpful here. Take the case of travelers returning home with accounts of a faraway country. Assume that it can be demonstrated beyond the shadow of a doubt that every one of these accounts is determined by the historical, socioeconomic, and psychological characteristics of the traveler in question. Thus one traveler sees the faraway country as a reflection of the past history of his own country, another describes it as the solution to the social problems from which he has suffered in his own life, another perceives it as the embodiment of his worst fears or best hopes. And so on and so forth. As the critical observer analyzes all these reports, it is perfectly plausible for him to perceive the faraway country as a gigantic projection of the travelers' own country. Indeed, the travelers' accounts will be very useful in gaining a better understanding of their home country. None of this, however, invalidates the proposition that the faraway country does indeed exist and that something about it can be gleaned from the travelers' accounts. The final point is not that Marco Polo was an Italian—and, who knows, an Italian with all sorts of class resentments and with an unresolved Oedipus complex—*but that he visited China.*

Modern philosophy and science, in the wake of Feuerbach, are quite correct in seeing religion as a symbolization of the human world. The gods are indeed symbols of human realities. This insight, important as it is, does not necessarily imply that the gods are *nothing but* that. Religious experience insists that, over and beyond their capacity to become human symbols, the gods inhabit a reality that is *sui generis* and that is sovereignly independent of what human beings project into it. What is more, religious experience suggests that the opposite understanding of the matter is finally the more important one: The human world in its entirety (including its various symbol systems) is itself a symbol—to wit, a symbol of the divine. In the most literal sense of "symbol," the human world *stands for* something beyond itself. It is a reflection, a signal, an intimation of another world. If men project their own meanings into the sky, their very capacity to do this comes from the fact that they have a celestial affinity. Feuerbach and all his successors have grasped only one side of this dialectic of man-as-symbol-

izer/man-as-symbol, man-as-projector/man-as-project. To grasp
the dialectic in its fullness is *ipso facto* to begin transcending
the boundaries of modern secular consciousness. It also means
to reject the reductive option for contemporary religious
thought.

5

The Inductive Possibility: From Tradition to Experience

EVERY TRADITION CONSISTS of frozen memories. And every questioning of tradition is likely to lead to an effort at unfreezing the memories. This is even true of individuals. An individual also develops minitraditions. Prominent among these are the traditions of youth, frozen somewhere along the line and then carried over in this fixated state into the later years of life. For example, a long-ago love affair is frozen into a limited number of images, like tableaux of the mind. Whenever the individual thinks about these events in the past or talks about them, it is these few images that are evoked in ritual fashion. Then something happens to put this construction in question—it no longer fits a new self-definition of the individual, or somebody comes up with a different version, or (worst of all) the long-lost love reappears in the flesh and forces the terrible question "How could I ever have been in love with *this* person?!" At that point, the individual becomes interested in taking the tradition apart, in looking at the evidence—old letters, say, or other written sources, or the recollections of witnesses who are still around. In other words, the individual is now embarked on an enterprise of trying to uncover the experiences that, long ago, came to be embodied in a tradition of youthful love.

Needless to say, this process of tracing a tradition back to the experiences that began it is more complex if the memories at issue are collective rather than individual ones. But the fundamental enterprise is the same. There will be, above all, the urge to find out "how it really was" (in the words of the German historian Ranke, *"wie es wirklich gewesen ist"*). As has been argued earlier in this book, the modern situation inevitably puts tradition in question, and by the same token releases an immense curiosity to find out "how it really was." The so-called subjectivism and empiricism of modern thought, its fascination with consciousness and with experience, thus has an inevitable dimension of history. It is no accident that the modern age has been called the age of "historism"; Hegel, in all likelihood, is the philosopher who represents "historicized" thought in its most sophisticated form, but he is by no means the only representative. Be this as it may, the roots of modern "historism" are existential rather than theoretical. The roots are in the cognitive requirements of a situation in which all memories appear unreliable and in which individuals, even very nonphilosophical ones, come to have a personal interest in knowing "how it really was." The subjectivization and historicization of religion in modern thought has the same roots.

As has also been argued before in this book, Protestantism underwent this process earlier and more thoroughly than any other religious tradition—for reasons that are due neither to some cognitive superiority nor to some cognitive defect of Protestants but quite simply to the peculiarly intimate relation of Protestantism to the genesis of the modern world. Thus Protestantism once more provides the best illustrations of a third possibility of coming to terms with the heretical imperative of the modern situation—the inductive possibility. The term "induction" is used here in its most common sense—arguing from empirical evidence. This means two things: taking human experience as the starting point of religious reflection, and using the methods of the historian to uncover those human experiences that have become embodied in the various religious traditions. Liberal Protestant theology has been marked above all by these two methodological principles, and, for this reason, should be of great interest even to people who could not care less about the substantive issues that have been troubling these Protestant theologians. The present interest too is primarily methodological. In other words, the inductive approach exemplified by Protestant liberalism will be looked at as *a possible model for thinking about religion*—not just about Christianity as modified by the Protestant Reformation but about *any* religion.

Back to Schleiermacher

It takes a paradigmatic figure to spot another one. Karl Barth, who was discussed in chapter 3 as the most illustrious example of the neo-orthodox option in modern Protestantism, characterized Friedrich Schleiermacher as the paradigmatic figure of Protestant liberalism. Indeed, throughout his work Barth was engaged in an ongoing dialogue with Schleiermacher (a dialogue, incidentally, in which Barth always treated his unseen opponent with very great respect and empathy). Few historians today would quarrel with Barth on this. Schleiermacher is indeed an overpowering figure, throwing his immense shadow over Protestant theology throughout the nineteenth century. And as we have noted—and as Barth also saw very correctly—the nineteenth century for Protestantism (as for many other components of Western civilization) ended not in 1900 but with World War I. The present argument will follow Barth's assessment in this matter. If one wants to understand the cognitive model of induction in its Protestant form, it is to Schleiermacher that one had best turn.[1]

Schleiermacher was a great revisionist. Revisionism is possible in all traditions, but Protestantism has, as it were, a built-in revisionist tendency.[2] The Protestant Reformation pitted itself against the authority of Rome by revising current tradition in the name of the Scriptures; the Reformers were thus compelled to go back to the sources of all Christian tradition—that is, to try to find out "how it really was." Also, the Reformers (Luther most dramatically) stood upon their right of conscience in defying traditional authority. In other words, both modern "historism" and modern subjectivism have, to say the least, intimate connections with Protestantism. In both these aspects Schleiermacher was very much a Protestant. In terms of his eighteenth-century background, Schleiermacher mobilized these ur-Protestant impulses to oppose the two predominant forms of religious thought of the day—a rigid Protestant orthodoxy on the one hand and Enlightenment rationalism on the other hand, both of which Schleiermacher regarded as arid and unsatisfactory. Needless to say, Schleiermacher's work had its contemporary influences (and also needless to say, scholars go on arguing which of these were the most important)— Pietism, with its emphasis on personal religious experience (Schleiermacher's origins were Calvinist, but he was reared in Pietist schools); the Romantic movement, with its emphasis on "feeling" (Gefühl), which after all is but another term for experience (Schleiermacher was a close friend of the Romantic Schelling); and Kantian philosophy, with its stress on the limits of reason and its quest for the a priori essence of things (it has been argued that Schleiermacher wanted to complete and correct Kant's work by writing a "critique of religion").

Yet Schleiermacher fused all these influences into a theoretical construction of sharp originality and vast intellectual power. His lifelong enterprise was a reformulation of Christian theology in terms of the human experience of faith.[3] Such a theology would be empirical (especially in the sense of a historical reconstruction of religious experience) and anthropological (as starting from commonly available human data). By the same token, such a theology may be called inductive.[4] Barth characterized this enterprise quite fairly as a theology of consciousness, and it is as such that it has become a negative paradigm for all neo-orthodox theologians in this century.[5] They were right in this (leaving aside details of interpretation or misinterpretation). If neo-orthodoxy means taking divine revelation rather than human experience as the starting point of religious reflection, then Schleiermacher's inductive approach is indeed the diametrically opposed alternative.

It is obviously impossible to give an overview here of Schleiermacher's complex and prolific opus. Only two of his works will be briefly looked at—his lectures *On Religion* (1799), which made him famous almost overnight, and the systematic work of his maturity *The Christian Faith* (1821). It goes without saying that even so only a few highlights of these two works can be brought out.

The lectures *On Religion* (subtitled *Speeches to the Cultured Among Its Despisers*) were given in Berlin before Schleiermacher had an academic appointment (he was a hospital chaplain). Even today, upon reading them, one is struck by their force and elegance.[6] From the beginning, they address themselves to the core question: What is the essence (*Wesen*) of religion? That essence is defined by Schleiermacher as the experience of the infinite or of God, also characterized as an experience of absolute dependence.[7] *This* is what religion is all about—*not* theoretical speculation, *nor* moral preachings. Doctrines and moral maxims are the result of reflection about religious experience and of the practical application of such experience—that is, they are only the outer garb of religion. The underlying experience of all religion, its essence, is one of encountering the infinite within the finite phenomena of human life. This encounter leaves man with a sense of absolute dependence or contingency, which is the awe that lies at the heart of the religious attitude. If one understands this central fact about religion, one moves away from "the childish operations of metaphysicians and moralists of religion."[8]

One of the basic criticisms that have been made of Schleiermacher has been to the effect that his method was the predecessor of Feuerbach's. It would be more accurate to say that Schleiermacher's method is the opposite of Feuerbach's. The latter, as was pointed out before, sought to reduce infinity to finitude, to translate theology into anthropology. Schleiermacher, by contrast, only uses an anthropological starting point in his theologizing, and he views the finite as being shot through with manifestations of the infinite. In his discussion of miracles (a tender topic in an intellectual milieu saturated with Enlightenment rationalism) he argues that the world is full of them, in the sense of *signs and intimations of the infinite* even in the most natural and common events.[9] Put in more recent terminology, the empirical universe is a symbol of the infinite, and it is "miraculous" in that it is ongoingly permeated with signals of the latter's transcendent reality. Schleiermacher's understanding of revelation (which of course greatly shocked all orthodox theologians) was in line with this, as it were, symbolic interpretation of empirical reality. He defines revelation as "every original and new disclosure of the universe and its innermost life to man."[10] It should be noted that implicit in this definition is the *plurality* of revelations, thus immediately challenging the "once and for all" self-understanding of every kind of orthodoxy.

Schleiermacher was fully conscious of the problematic character of this view for any Christian (or, *mutatis mutandis*, anyone with a faith commitment to any specific revelation). His fourth lecture, essentially a sort of precocious treatise in the sociology of religion, deals with the way in which religious experience comes to be embodied in a human community.[11] These sociological considerations lead directly and logically to the simple fact that there are *many* such communities of faith—the topic dealt with in the fifth lecture.[12] The multiplicity of religious forms is the natural consequence of the core experience of religion. But this does not mean that all forms are equally valid or should be regarded only as interim manifestations of the divine. The Enlightenment notion of a common, universal "natural religion" is a pale abstraction and empirically inadequate in its view of the concrete religious forms (the "positive religions") of human history. So far, so good. But now Schleiermacher must deal with the obvious question of how one is to assess the validity of any particular religious form (and *ipso facto* of the revelation it purports to embody).

Schleiermacher proposes a method of inquiry by which every religion, even if it has degenerated into empty rituals and abstract theories, is traced back to its experiential source. This method is both historical and phenomenological. It allows the discovery that "all the dead embers were once glowing effusions of inner fire."[13] As these experiences of "inner fire" come once again into view, it becomes possible to assess the specific forms of religion as being closer to or farther away from the core experience of God. In other words, the historical and phenomenological operations (tracing taditions back to their original ex-

periences, and grasping the essence of these experiences)
constitute the prelude to the theological operation proper,
which must seek to assess the truth claims of the revelations in
question.

In the context of the present book it is noteworthy that
Schleiermacher actually calls this method one of "heresy":
"Every specific form of religion . . . is a particular positive
religion. [It is thus] in relation to the totality of religious
phenomena—to use a word that should be rehabilitated—*a
heresy* [*eine Haeresis*], because among many equals one is, so
to speak, chosen to be the head of the others"![14] Schleiermacher thus confronts what has here been called the heretical
imperative with incisive clarity. He also pursues, without flinch-
ing, the question of why one should choose Christianity as
against another one of the "positive religions." Christianity is
compared with other religions, which are described in very one-
sided ways (for instance, there is a long discussion of the
"stunted" character of Judaism, which few historians today
would endorse). Christianity is then affirmed as "the most perfect idealization" of religion.[15] The superiority of Christianity
is principally derived from its "idea" of Christ as the mediator,
an "idea" that perfectly expresses the presence of the infinite
within the finite. This christocentric aspect of Schleiermacher's
theology is remarkable, in view of the criticisms that have been
directed against it.

The essence of the specifically Christian religious experience,
then, is the "idea" of Christ as the mediator between God and
man; in terms of Schleiermacher's own methodology, the term
"idea" must *not* be taken in an abstract, theoretical sense;
"core motif" might be a better term to use today.[16] In any case,
"idea" refers to the essence of the Christian *experience*. The
Christian Scriptures have authority only insofar as they are the
most important testimony of this experience. Schleiermacher

asserts that these particular writings became scripture "out of
their own strength"—and adds, with breathtaking liberality,
that other writings could join them if they evinced the same
strength![17]

The bold outline of a theological approach presented by
Schleiermacher in the speeches of 1799 finally led to the elegant system of the dogmatics of 1821; by the same token, the
latter work, *The Christian Faith*, may be seen as the climax of
Schleiermacher's "heretical" enterprise.[18] The entire range of
classical Christian doctrine is reorganized here in terms of
Schleiermacher's inductive method. In other words, every proposition deriving from the Christian tradition is traced back to
specific religious experiences which, supposedly, were at the
roots of the tradition. Now it must be stressed that this
methodological procedure can be looked at in separation from
the substantive arguments that Schleiermacher makes. And
looking at it in this way, of course, is the present interest. Thus
one may be interested in Schleiermacher's method without necessarily accepting the results to which, in his opinion, the
method led. That method, more clearly and comprehensively
now than in *On Religion*, is grounded in the analysis of
religious experience in general and Christian religious experience in particular.

The essence of religion is neither theoretical knowledge nor
practical activity (such as moral actions) but a particular kind
of experience. This experience is now described as "an immediate self-consciousness."[19] This, of course, can be described as a
form of subjectivism, but that term must be carefully applied.
At no point does Schleiermacher maintain that religious experience is *nothing but* human self-consciousness. On the contrary,
he insists that religious consciousness is consciousness *of something beyond itself*—indeed, so much beyond itself that the
human subject feels himself to be utterly dependent on that

other reality or being at the center of the experience. In other words, to start with human consciousness does not mean that one must also end there; on the contrary, in Schleiermacher's case, human consciousness is of interest to the theologian only insofar as it bears the marks, the "intimations," of a God who is utterly beyond human measure.[20] Again, the experience of absolute dependence is designated as the core experience of religion.

The "pious self-consciousness" which is the result of religious experience must necessarily be expressed in collective forms, or "pious communities." The Christian church is but one such community, formed by the specific characteristics of Christian religious experience. More amply now than in the earlier work, the superiority of Christianity among the world religions is argued in developmental (or, if one wills, evolutionary) terms. There are different stages in the development of human religion. Within the generally higher stage of monotheism, Christianity is the most perfect form of religion. This does not mean, however, that all the other forms are false; rather, they are not only necessary stages but partial insights into the religious constitution of the universe. The perfection of Christianity is then argued again by an essentially pejorative comparison with other religions, but also (and this is methodologically more important) by focusing on the redemptive character of Christ. In other words, Christianity is the most developed religion because of what it has to say about Jesus Christ. This Christian message of salvation touches upon the deepest human needs. Schleiermacher's peculiar combination of christocentrism and consciousness-analysis produced a strongly dualistic organization for most of the work: There are, on the one hand, long analyses of the human condition and of human consciousness as being in need of redemption (as in the treatment of the doctrine of sin) and, on the other hand, discussions of

divine redemptive activity answering this need. Thus there is
no contradiction in Schleiermacher's procedure: This entire
work is organized in terms of the contents of Christian "pious
self-consciousness"—but since those contents all focus on Jesus
Christ, the work is also radically christocentric!

It also follows from this methodology that there must be no
confusion between the levels of religious experience and religious theorizing, between faith and dogma. Experience is prior
to all theories about it. This insight protects Schleiermacher
from the dogmatism of Protestant orthodoxy. It is for this
reason, of course, that he gave his systematic work the title he
did. It is also noteworthy, though, that the subtitle of the work
is *According to the Principles of the Evangelical Church*. In
other words, Schleiermacher's method did not lead him into a
theological position divorced from any tradition or community.
He remained deeply committed to the German Protestant
church, served it as a preacher all his life, and indeed cele-
brated communion with his family on his very deathbed. In retrospect, the twentieth-century observer is unlikely to be persuaded by Schleiermacher's arguments for the superiority of
Christianity. But neither will the observer be persuaded by
Schleiermacher's critics that his method leads into a night in
which all cats are gray, in which Christianity is dissolved into a
general and inevitably pallid notion of religion. Both Schleiermacher's thought and life contradict this conclusion.

An Inductive Model

It is not difficult to look on Schleiermacher's work as a
model of the inductive possibility in modern religious thought
—not only because it contains in particularly lucid form the
crucial ingredients of this approach but also because in actual

fact Schleiermacher's approach served as a model for Protestant theology for well over a century. It is not an exaggeration to say that, until the appearance of Barthian neo-orthodoxy in the 1920s, Protestant theology after Schleiermacher was one long struggle with his ghost (especially, but not only, in the German-speaking countries). Protestant theological liberalism has been characterized in different ways, but it is defensible to maintain that at its core is the inductive method that Schleiermacher first developed. Put differently, if there is one central category of Protestant theological liberalism, it is the category of religious experience (though, as has already been pointed out, various terms were used to denote this). The core of the inductive model is, quite simply, the assertion that a specific type of human experience defines the phenomenon called religion. This experience can be described and analyzed. Any theoretical reflection about religion (including the theoretical enterprise of theology) must begin with religious experience (so that, for theology, the unavoidable procedure is to go from the human to the metahuman, and not in the reverse direction). Just as there is a fundamental religious experience, there is also a multiplicity of religious forms in history. Each one is to be described and analyzed in terms of its essence, so that an investigation of the truth claims of any one of these religious forms must be grounded in comparative and historical analysis. Christianity is not an exception to this. It is one of the historically available religious forms, analyzable by the same empirical and phenomenological methods as all the other forms. Whatever truth claims are then made for Christianity, and on whatever grounds, they must be able to stand up to the scrutiny of inductive reasoning. In other words, Christian theology cannot occur in a sanctuary that provides immunity from the questions of historical science and of the other empirical disciplines. The aim to carry on the business of theologizing in precisely such a sanctuary is the hard differentiating criterion between theological liberalism and its orthodox as well as neo-orthodox adversaries: Theological liberals deny the validity and feasibility of this aim; orthodox as well as neo-orthodox continue to aspire to it.

The immense historiographical contributions of nineteenth-century Protestant scholarship can be understood as one important part of Schleiermacher's heritage. Given the inductive premise, it became urgently important to establish as accurately as possible "how it really was"—in the history of ancient Israel, of the early Christian community, and of the developing Christian church ever since. Given the same inductive premise, the Protestant scholar not only had a motive to find out "how it really was" but also had a theological self-understanding that allowed him to take the risks of such an intellectual undertaking. This is why the great majority of these scholars, even when they came upon historical facts that were highly disturbing to orthodoxy (this was especially the case with biblical scholarship), could remain within the Protestant community, in many cases as ordained preachers, without compromising their intellectual integrity. By the same token, this vast enterprise of historical scholarship continually interacted with the formulations of systematic theology. Indeed, systematic theology itself became a primarily historical discipline—or at least a deeply history-conscious discipline.

The school of Albrecht Ritschl was the principal embodiment of the historical impulse in Protestant theology in this era.[21] But a later individual may be seen as the single most representative figure in this line, namely Adolf von Harnack.[22] A historian of dogma and author of what is still the definitive history of the development of Christian doctrine, Harnack's vast work of scholarly reconstruction flows directly from Schleiermacher's inductive premise. Harnack painted the gigan-

138 *The Heretical Imperative*

tic canvas of Christian history in order to show how, over and over again, the essence of Christianity reasserted itself in different historical situations and linked up in many ways with different human cultures. This quest for the essence (*Wesen*) of Christianity is, as was shown before, of key importance in the inductive model. The most successful expression of this quest by Harnack was an enormously popular work appropriately enough entitled *The Essence of Christianity*.[23] This work was based on academic lectures given by Harnack in Berlin exactly one hundred years after Schleiermacher addressed the "cultured despisers of religion" in exactly the same location. Harnack's lectures of 1899, like Schleiermacher's of 1799, tried to accomplish two things—to describe Christianity as an empirical human reality and to defend its truth claims despite (or even because of) this description. The not inconsiderable difference was that Harnack could now marshal the results of a century of historical scholarship for his theological purposes. As in Schleiermacher, the historical interest of Harnack's work is finally directed to the experiences underlying the various theoretical developments.[24] In other words, the overall historiographical enterprise and the quest for the essence of Christianity are closely interwoven.

Schleiermacher's influence in the field of religion was not limited to Protestant theology, although it is most dominant there. The same inductive approach, with its interest in comparisons and in phenomenological description of essences, was also powerfully expressed in nontheological religious scholarship. A case can be made that Schleiermacher was also the father of the disciplines of comparative religion and history of religion (*Religionsgeschichte*) in the nineteenth century, disciplines that have enormously magnified the knowledge available on every expression of human religiosity. Schleiermacher is certainly at the methodological roots of what came to be known in the twentieth century as the phenomenology of religion. Its foremost representative if not founder, Rudolf Otto (whose work was discussed in chapter 2), acknowledged his indebtedness to Schleiermacher.

The inductive approach in Protestant theology was, as was discussed earlier, sharply challenged in the wake of the Barthian revolution. Of course it did not disappear in the decades of neo-orthodox dominance, but it seemed passé to those who thought of themselves as the theological vanguard in Protestantism. It is now possible, in retrospect, to say that this assessment was mistaken. Since World War II there has been a strong resurgence of trends that must be seen in continuity with the classical liberal tradition. This is not the place to trace these developments, but the work of Paul Tillich in this country and of Wolfhart Pannenberg in Germany should at least be mentioned in this connection. Neo-orthodoxy was not the end but an interruption of the development of liberal theology. This, in the perspective of the present argument, is not only what one would expect sociologically; it is also what one should welcome theologically.

Criticisms of the Model

If the last statement is to be maintained, the criticisms made of classical liberal theology will have to be confronted—all the more so as most of these criticisms would apply, mutatis mutandis, to other versions of the inductive model. Again, this can only be done briefly here. But it should be said right away that, while some of the criticisms must be conceded, the positive position on the continuing viability of the model will not be abandoned.

The inductive model, by its very nature, occupies a middle

ground, a position of compromise. This is a vulnerable position, often a transitory one. Very often the theologian who begins with an inductive approach ends up with formulations that are hard to distinguish from reductionism. Possibly the best illustration of this was the strong tendency of Protestant liberals in the nineteenth century to identify the essence of Christianity with ethics or with the cultural achievements of Western civilization. The American form of this, by the way, is still very much alive in the identification of Christianity either with ordinary morality or (a little less frequently today) with the social ideals of the "American way of life." In its full-blown forms, needless to say, such an understanding of the essence of Christianity is tantamount to a secularizing reduction. Thus, what Christianity is "really all about" turns out to be this or that set of values that are perfectly consonant with the prevailing secular consciousness—the values of humanistic ethics (however specified), of Western man, or of American democracy. While it must be conceded that there were indeed cases in which the essence of Christianity, or of religion as such, was secularized in this fashion, this was not always the case, especially not in the work of the greatest representatives of Protestant liberalism. Thus Schleiermacher, Ritschl, and Harnack all emphasized ethics as well as cultural achievements in their discussions of the merits of Christianity, but none of the three *identified* Christianity with these ethical and cultural merits. More importantly, there is no intrinsic reason why an inductive model would have to slide over into reductionism: The best guarantee against this happening is that the procedures used within the model really be inductive, and meticulously so. The earlier discussion of religious experience in this book should make clear why this statement can be made here with some assurance.

Perhaps more rare was the opposite loss of the middle

ground—the sliding over of induction into an orthodox or neo-orthodox position. It is found in a variety of liberal theologians who carried the inductive impulse up to a point—and then stopped, turned around, and declared whatever topics had been left out to be objects of faith in the authority of revelation and *ipso facto* immune to inductive reasoning. This was certainly not the case with Schleiermacher or Harnack, though Ritschl might be characterized as having done so. But, again, there is no intrinsic reason why an inductive model would have to come up against such an irreducible remnant of the tradition before which only submission to authority is possible. No element of a religious tradition is immune to inductive reasoning. This does *not* mean that inductive reasoning can ever *prove* the truth claim of an alleged revelation in the way a natural science proves or validates its hypotheses. In that final sense, religious affirmations always entail faith. But there is no reason why such faith must mean arresting the course of inductive reasoning. On the contrary, one's own faith and the experiences brought on by this faith will actually constitute "data" or "evidence" upon which inductive reflection can take place. Properly understood, faith and inductive reasoning stand in a dialectical relation to each other: I believe—and I then reflect about the implications of this fact; I gather evidence about that which is the object of my faith—and this evidence provides a further motive to go on believing. This, of course, is a very different dialectic from the one taught by the Barthians: mellower, undoubtedly less inspiring—but also less demanding of a sacrifice of intellect, less conducive to fanaticism. And reasonableness has its own inspirations.

A related criticism has already been discussed above in connection with Schleiermacher—the criticism that the anthropological starting point must lead to a reduction of theology to anthropology in the manner of Feuerbach. As has been argued above, the criticism does not hold with Schleiermacher; even less can it be maintained that such a reduction is the necessary consequence of any inductive approach in religious thought. In a broader sense, the criticism is to the effect that a focus on the human reality of religious experience must lead to an endless subjectivism, devoid of any objective criteria. The end result of such subjectivism would then be an attitude to religion in which anything goes: I believe because it feels good—or, I choose to believe, and I refuse to argue about the grounds of my choice. In other words, the anthropological starting point is criticized as bringing forth either psychologism or "decisionism," or both, with regard to religious affirmations. Again, it cannot be denied that such developments have indeed issued from Protestant theological liberalism; in American Protestantism one can easily parade an array of horrible examples of this kind. Nor can one deny the possibility, perhaps even probability, that similar aberrations would issue from other versions of the inductive model. But, again, this is not a necessary development, and there are ways of guarding against it. The most important safeguard is a clear understanding of the intentionality of religious consciousness: Religious experience is indeed a human experience, but by its very nature it intends the metahuman. A truly inductive approach will take cognizance of both the human reality and the metahuman intentionality of the religious phenomenon.

There is a more sociological, or even political, aspect of this criticism: The liberal understanding of religion as a complement and a culmination of the human has been criticized as leading to a legitimation of the social-cultural and political status quo. On the level of actual history, this criticism is well founded. Classical theological liberalism did indeed issue in so-called *Kulturprotestantismus*, by which the social, cultural, and political structures of the nineteenth century were given a sort of theological baptism.[25] Revulsion against this facile identification of Christianity with whatever happened to be around sociologically was, of course, an important motive for the revolts against theological liberalism from Kierkegaard to Barth. The latter eloquently described his revulsion upon finding that almost all his great liberal teachers, including Harnack, fell prey to the patriotic war hysteria of 1914. A few years later this Barthian point of view seemed to be validated by the efficacy of Barthian theology in the Christian resistance to Nazism. Yet, upon closer scrutiny, this argument is less persuasive than it may seem at first. To be sure, theological liberalism may lead to the legitimation of this or that status quo. But one glance at church history will quickly reveal that this sociological function has been shared by every conceivable form of Christian theology, including the grimmest orthodoxics. As to Barthian neo-orthodoxy, it should be given every credit for its historical nexus with Christian anti-Nazism. But it is not irrelevant to observe that many of the same theologians who were so clear-sighted about Nazism (Barth emphatically among them) were singularly obtuse when it came to understanding Communism after 1945. Indeed, in a number of places it can be argued that Barthianism became a legitimating ideology for the new status quo of Communist totalitarianism. In terms of the sociology of religion it is plausible to propose that the legitimating function is deeply ingrained in institutional religion (for reasons that cannot be developed here), irrespective of the prevailing forms of religious thought. It is further plausible to propose that reversals of this function—that is, cases where religion served to delegitimate the status quo—have taken place under greatly varying theological auspices. In sum, *no particular theological position guarantees social or political clear-sightedness.* Put differently, *sociological obtuseness can be found on every point of the theological spectrum.* To this, of course, must be added the more basic observation that sociopolitical perspicacity is not in itself a criterion of theological method. As an analogy, even if one could demonstrate that Copernicus was an absolute fool with regard to the social realities of his age, this demonstration would not strengthen the theory that the earth is flat and that the sun moves around it.

There is the criticism that theological liberalism gets caught in the "merely historical"—that is, that the individual will go on asking "how it really was" and forego the more important religious questions, "Is this true?" and "Do I believe this?" Against this attitude of being caught in the "merely historical" Kierkegaard developed his notion of "contemporaneity"— across the gulf of what he called "the nineteen hundred years," the individual must place himself once more in the position of Jesus' contemporaries and confront in his own existence the staggering claims of Jesus' message. Leave aside here the questions of whether such Kierkegaardian "contemporaneity" is really possible, or whether many orthodox or neo-orthodox affirmations would survive this confrontation with the historical Jesus. The more basic weakness of this criticism is that it is directed not against theological liberalism as such but rather against *any* form of arid intellectualism. In this regard, being caught in historical problems is no worse, religiously speaking, than being caught in dogmatic problems. On the contrary, it is precisely an approach that respects history that is most likely to lead to a modicum of "contemporaneity," be it with Jesus or with any other empirical manifestation of religious truth. It was Ranke, the historian, who said that every age is immediate to God; historical scholarship, more than any other discipline, is instrumental in retrieving this immediacy out of the dying embers of tradition.

And then there are various criticisms of Protestant theological liberalism in terms of its untenable historical assumptions.

These must be conceded in bulk, as it were. Thus the classical liberal theologians often operated with an empirically falsifiable idea of religious evolution. They had sometimes grotesquely distortive notions of non-Christian religions. Most of them had notions about the teachings of Jesus and about early Christian ethics that have been disproved, probably conclusively, by more recent New Testament scholarship. For example (and it is a rather crucial example), not only has it been shown that Jesus had no ethical teachings that differed appreciably from the ethics of contemporary Judaism but more importantly that neither he nor his early disciples had much interest in ethical teachings of any sort. It follows that any interpretation of the essence of Christianity in terms of ethics must be mistaken. One could easily compile a list of such historical errors. But none of these criticisms touch the methodological principles of theological liberalism. It is the latter principles that, it is argued in this book, continue to be viable—*not* the various historical interpretations made by the classical liberal theologians. In sum, *no specific errors of induction invalidate the inductive method.* Analogically, if a chemist makes even a terrible mistake in a laboratory experiment, the proper correction of this mistake is to repeat the experiment in the most painstaking way possible —*not* to overturn the methodology of chemistry or to deny its status as a scientific discipline.

The Quest for Certainty and Its Frustrations

Even if the preceding criticisms of classical theological liberalism are rejected there remain three persistent problems of this approach in religious thought—problems that will recur in any new version of the inductive model. The three problems are, when all is said and done, aspects of the one general problem posed by the heretical imperative. But it is convenient to speak here of three distinct problems: The problem of "false" religious experience; the problem of the status of one's preferred historical religion; and the problem of religious certainty.

The problem of "false" religious experience is not new. For example, the prophets of Yahweh in ancient Israel were frequently plagued by the competition of "false prophets"—and the religious public was plagued by the, as it were, epistemological problem of how to differentiate "true" from "false" prophecy. The Hebrew Bible is not much help in supplying criteria. For one thing, religious history, like all history, is written by the victors, who naturally present their own favorites as the "true" spokesmen for the founding revelation. Apart from that, the populace, it seems, bestowed the quality of "true prophecy" on those characters who could produce the most fireworks, be it by miraculous deeds or by the sort of personal magnetism that is now called charisma. Neither is very cogent as a criterion. Suppose that Elijah had failed in his famous meteorological experiment on Mount Carmel or that he had been less of a charismatic personality: Would that have validated the religious experience of the Baalim as against that of Yahweh? And so on.

William James, an explicit advocate of an inductive approach to religion, was very conscious of this problem. In the chapter entitled "The Reality of the Unseen" in his classic *The Varieties of Religious Experience* James recounts miscellaneous reports of contacts with God, then exclaims, "Such is the human ontological imagination, and such is the convincingness of what it brings to birth."[26] James offers at least two answers to the problem in his classic work, and the two are not very coherently related to each other. The first answer, given early in the book, is most consistent with James's overall philosophical position of pragmatism: The test of religious belief is "the way in which it works on the whole"—that is, the criterion of a religious truth claim is its "fruits."[27] For this position, which he calls "empiricist," James enlists the support of such discrepant authorities as Saint Teresa of Avila and Jonathan Edwards (each in her/his way an exponent of "experimental religion"). James assumed that the "fruits" of religious experience were moral. This assumption is troublesome: Is morality ever a good criterion for truth claims of *any* kind? And if not, as seems pretty evident from the history of human thought, why should religion be an exception? Thus the theory of relativity would not be one iota less persuasive if Einstein had been a moral monster instead of the morally admirable individual he actually was—and, conversely, the theory of relativity did not gain one iota of persuasiveness by the admirable moral qualities of its author. It is possible to argue, of course, that religion is a different case, because God is the ultimately moral being and would not reveal his truths to or through grossly immoral human beings. The argument is weak. Few of history's great "religious virtuosi" (to use Max Weber's term) are very attractive figures in human or moral terms. Are their statements about the "reality of the unseen" to be discounted for this reason?

James seems to have felt the shakiness of his moralistic criterion, and later in his great book the notion of "fruits" shifts from ethical to cognitive results Thus in his discussion of mysticism, with its uncomfortable proximity to the "accumulated traditions . . . which the text-books on insanity supply," James points out that the same mental region from which mystical insights spring also contains every variety of mad illusion. He then goes on: "That region contains every kind of matter: 'seraph and snake' abide there side by side. To come from thence is no infallible credential. What comes must be sifted and tested, and run the gauntlet of confrontation with the total context of experience, just like what comes from the outer world of sense. Its value must be ascertained by empirical methods, so long as we are not mystics ourselves."[28] Leave aside here the question of whether things would be all that different if we *were* mystics ourselves (poor Teresa of Avila, for one, was much troubled by devilish voices which pretended to come from God and which, apparently, often convinced her for a while). Be this as it may, the criterion for the alleged insights of religious experience here is cognitive rather than moral. The "sifting and testing" of these insights is precisely the process that al-Ghazali talked about when he described reason as God's scale on earth and insisted that the wild proclamations of the mystics be put on this scale. Needless to say, the scale is not infallible, nor does it provide very accurate measures. But the only way of even beginning to tell "true" from "false" religious experience is to weigh the insights purporting to come from the experience on the scale of reason. What is more, James is quite correct in calling this procedure "empiricist," in the sense that religious experience must be assessed in the context of all other human experiences and all other empirical knowledge about the human condition.

Let there be no misunderstanding about this formulation: The last thing in the world it is intended to imply is the stance of Enlightenment rationalism with regard to religion—that stance *against* which Schleiermacher developed his method. The core of the religious phenomenon, as Rudolf Otto understood very clearly, is beyond all rationality. And, as James put it, all rational reflection about religion is "like translations of a text into another tongue."[29] But, inadequate as this may be for the deeply rooted human urge for "infallible credentials" in this area, nothing better can be suggested than sober rational assessment in the matter of finding criteria for distinguishing "true" religious experience from its flawed imitations.

Then, there is the persistent problem of the basis on which an inductive model of religious thought could prefer one revelation (in Schleiermacher's sense of the term) over another. Put differently, if there is a heretical imperative, why go for one heresy rather than another? In classical Protestant liberalism, of course, this question was identical with the question of the privileged status of Christianity (and, to a somewhat lesser degree, of the status of Protestantism). Schleiermacher's approach to this question has already been indicated. In the more recent period of liberal theology, the question was a central concern in the work of Ernst Troeltsch.[30] The question was put by Troeltsch as that of the "absoluteness" of Christianity, and his answer, in a book with just that title, may be taken as paradigmatic for this type of theological thinking.[31]

Both history and sociology (the two disciplines in which Troeltsch undertook virtually all of his scholarly work—in the latter, by the way, under the strong influence of Max Weber) are schools of relativity. Qua historian and sociologist, Troeltsch accepted fully that this relativity extended to religion. Qua Christian theologian, however, he had to confront the question of the manner in which the absolute truth claims of Christianity could be maintained within an ocean of relativizations. Methodologically (and here Weber's influence is very evident) he was certain that such absoluteness could not be established scientifically, nor could it be established by placing Christianity at the top rung of some Hegelian or quasi-Hegelian evolutionary ladder. Christianity is a historical phenomenon like any other, analyzable by historical and sociological methods like any other. In other words, as a historical phenomenon, Christianity is a relative phenomenon, for "the historical and the relative are identical."[32]

This relativity is not endless, but is reducible to some major types of religious possibilities in history. Indeed, Troeltsch argued that, if one goes beyond the multiplicity of primitive forms, there are the two opposing types of the monotheistic religions of western Asia and the great religious traditions of India. The essential alternative is between these two types. This important point will be taken up again in the next chapter of the present book. But, be this as it may, for Troeltsch the procedure to follow is for historical scholarship to clarify just what the great alternatives are, *after which* it is the task of the theologian or philosopher of religion to find a normative measure that will transcend the "merely historical" comparison. This normative measure can only come out of the free struggle between religious ideas; it cannot be deduced from some religious theory a priori, nor can it be the direct result of empirical analysis. In the end, this will be a matter of subjective decision by individuals who are rooted in a particular tradition but have also become open toward all the others.

A normative standard will have to assume comparability; that is, it presupposes that all religions have something in common and something generally valid. Troeltsch maintains that all religions tend toward a common goal. This goal is realized in stronger or weaker degree by different historical forms of religion. All religions relate to revelations of what Troeltsch calls a "higher life" (Eliade's term "hierophanies" would be appropriate here). Thus all religions tend toward and intend the absolute, but this absolute is never empirically available, never a safe possession. Rather, it is always there as an intuition, an intimation.[33] Only in this manner can any truth claim be made for Christianity. But such truth claims *can* be made, Troeltsch insists—calmly and confidently, understanding Christianity to be a historically relative form of religion but one which nevertheless has a unique and uniquely valid relation to the absolute.[34]

This, of course, once more entails a quest for the essence

(*Wesen*) of Christianity, in the manner of Schleiermacher and Harnack. The substantive details of this, especially in terms of the characterization of the non-Christian alternatives, are debatable; here Troeltsch is open to the same criticisms discussed above. But these substantive details are not of concern here; what is of concern is Troeltsch's method. And the latter is central to the inductive model as understood in the present argument. Within this model, the solution to the problem of the, so to speak, grounds for heresy will have to be sought along Troeltsch's lines.[35]

Finally, every inductive model will have to confront the persistent problem of certainty—in James's words, the problem of the profound religious urge for "infallible credentials." This problem nagged all the classical Protestant liberals and their alleged failure to provide an adequate solution was one of the important causes of the neo-orthodox revolt against liberalism. Barth and his friends in the early neo-orthodox movement confronted the problem first of all as preachers. Sunday after Sunday they were expected to mount the pulpit and proclaim some sort of Christian message in tones of confidence. Did theological liberalism make such tones possible? Or, as they put it, "how can this be preached?" There is a serious existential problem for such individuals, who are on the one hand committed to an inductive approach to religion and on the other hand institutionally commissioned to affirm the truth of a particular religious tradition. The problem, of course, is not limited to Protestant preachers; *mutatis mutandis*, it afflicts the official representatives of any religious tradition that has become the object of reflection and scrutiny. This problem cannot be addressed here. Suffice it to say that the problem is not insoluble. But the problem in its basic sense is not limited to this special category of religious professionals. Indeed, one might argue that it is even more pressing for the lay person, who does not have the intellectual tools of the theologically trained to cope with such questions and who nevertheless needs to feel certain of what the tradition proclaims as truth.

In principle, the quest for religious certainty is bound to be frustrated "in this world," except for momentary experiences that can only be maintained precariously in recollection. This principle follows with some necessity from the understanding of religious experience expounded in chapter 2 of this book. Put in phenomenological terms, there are indeed experiences of contact with the supernatural that carry within them absolute certainty, but this certainty is located only within the enclave of religious experience itself. As soon as the individual returns from this enclave into the world of ordinary everyday reality, this certainty is retained only as a memory and as such is intrinsically fragile. This is true even of those individuals who claim to have had the most intense encounters with the divine—mystics, say, or prophets, or others to whom the gods are supposed to have spoken directly. Mystical ecstasies or prophetic revelations are occurrences within specific time spans. These time spans come to an end and the individual willy-nilly goes back to what Alfred Schutz has called the "standard time" of common human life. The world literature of religion is full of complaints about this problem of maintaining the sense of the extraordinary within the realities of the ordinary. This is why there is the necessity of faith even for those who have directly experienced the "reality of the unseen." Such individuals, needless to say, are far and few between. For the rest of mankind the problem is even more intractable. It is doubly intractable for those who have tasted of the relativizing fruits of modern reflectiveness, for they are likely to be barred from the practical solution of the intellectually naïve—the blind, taken-for-granted adherence to their particular tradition. Yet even intellectuals have a need for certainty.

Troeltsch was also greatly troubled by this problem. He

asked whether the very restricted notion of absoluteness that, he asserted, was the necessary consequence of historical reflection could suffice for the religious needs of human beings. His answer was positive. Piety requires truth, but not necessarily in the old sense of absoluteness. The conviction that one has encountered God and heard his voice is not touched by the relativizations of historical consciousness. There are these encounters that carry within them an intrinsic conviction of truth. The individual can find certainty in this conviction. Even if he enters into the full gamut of historical and social-scientific relativizations, he can be confident that what has been experienced as truth by himself, and what has proven itself as truth in the lives of many other human beings, will never come to be seen as untruth. While there is no finality to any experience of truth in history, there is an unfolding process in which each instance of access to truth (each "hierophany," if one prefers) is preserved and carried forward. Put differently, piety requires certainty, but not fanaticism.[36]

This is how Troeltsch sums up his position on this problem: "There is now no longer the passionate fanaticism, which sees every challenge to exclusive absoluteness as a threat to everything believed in. Instead there is the mellow certainty that the authentic and true forces of reality will reassert themselves even in a wider context."[37] There is no better phrase than "mellow certainty" to describe the fundamental attitude of liberal theology at its best, and *ipso facto* the religious possibility that can be most happily combined with the inductive approach.

In Defense of Mellowness

The effort has been made in this book to be fair to each one of the three possibilities for religion discussed in the preceding chapters. Fairness has not meant neutrality. The argument is intended to lead to the proposition that the inductive possibility is the most viable of the three options—indeed, when all is said and done, the only viable option. Within the context of Christian theology, this means an unambiguous identification with the line of liberal Protestantism that originated with Schleiermacher. Within the broader context of religious pluralism, it means the opinion that the inductive model developed by the classical Protestant liberals holds promise for quite other traditions as well. As was stated repeatedly, this does not mean an endorsement of all the substantive positions of liberal Protestantism, especially not those that betray ethnocentric bias against the non-Western religions (not to mention Judaism and even the Catholic branches of Christianity). The endorsement, in other words, is solely methodological. That, though, is endorsing quite a lot, as has been shown.

On the contemporary theological scene a revitalization of liberal religion means a fruitful third option between the neo-orthodox reconstructions on the "right" and the capitulations to secularism on the "left" (the two terms here are used theologically rather than politically, of course—there are Barthian socialists and secularist advocates of American capitalism!). Against the right, this position means a reassertion of the human as the only possible starting point for theological reflection and a rejection of any external authority (be it scriptural, ecclesiastical, or traditional) that would impose itself on such reflection. Against the left, the position means a reassertion of the supernatural and sacred character of religious experience, and a rejection of the particularly oppressive authority of modern secular consciousness. This may sound like taking on a lot. Perhaps so, but there is no reason to think that those who take such a position will find themselves in an isolated situation.

This option, like any other, has its own plausibility structures. It is likely that the "mellowness" endemic to it will be more plausible in times of at least relative normality than in the midst of crisis. In times of crisis for society, and in moments when an individual is in what Karl Jaspers has called "marginal situations," fanaticisms tend to be more plausible. Thus it is no accident that Protestant liberalism flourished in Germany in the self-confident era preceding World War I, was severely shaken in the turbulent years between 1918 and 1945, and achieved a new lease on life as a new normality appeared in the wake of the West German "economic miracle." Such observations are the bread and butter of the sociologist of knowledge. It is all the more important to stress that the latter's analyses have no necessary bearing on the truth claims at issue: *The category of plausibility structure has no epistemological status whatever.*

Individuals who found themselves in political opposition to Nazi totalitarianism in the 1930s were in no mood to be mellow even in their intellectual positions. Neither are individuals today who feel morally committed to this or that revolutionary struggle. In such situations there is a great attraction to the apodictic affirmations of theological neo-orthodoxy or of revolutionary ideologies that are but secularized versions of religious dogmatism. This is very understandable, but one should not be overly impressed. To be sure, a person facing political persecution or the perils of war has insights that are denied to those who have not had such experiences. Similarly, there are distinctive insights that derive from experiences of personal sorrow, illness, or the proximity of death. But these insights out of "marginal situations," important though they may be, are not the only insights. The marginal situation as such as no *privileged* access to reality. Indeed, the marginal situation, by its very character, may obscure aspects of reality that can be seen more clearly in less desperate circumstances. Put simply, even if it were empirically correct that there are no atheists in foxholes, this would not be an argument for the existence of God. It follows that the insights of both types of situation must be assessed without prejudging their possible validity on sociological grounds.[38]

This is not intended to say that liberal religion can *only* flourish in times of tranquillity. On the contrary, there is a kind of mellowness that comes out of great inner strength. And apodictic certainties have a way of collapsing overnight. One could even suggest that those who have truly encountered the "reality of the unseen" can *afford* the mellowness of liberality, both in their lives and in their thinking.

6

Between Jerusalem
and Benares:
The Coming Contestation
of Religions

"WHAT IS ATHENS to Jerusalem?" asked Tertullian, the same Latin church father who, in his sour anti-Hellenism, was pleased to confess that he believed because it was absurd to do so. The implied answer to his question, of course, was "Nothing!" One may say that the entire history of Christianity provides the answer to Tertullian's question, an answer quite the opposite from the one he himself implied. Athens has been an awful lot of things to Jerusalem, beginning with the daring prologue to the Gospel of John, in which the Greek idea of the *logos* is identified with the Jewish Messiah—adumbrating a world-shattering marriage of reason and revelation, of universalism and the particularities of west-Asian religious experience. Indeed, one may even say with some justice that the history of Christianity has been, in essence, the story of the marriage of

Athens and Jerusalem. This does not mean, of course, that there have been no tensions between the Hellenic and the Israelite elements in the Christian synthesis. There have been such tensions, and to that extent Tertullian was not altogether wrong. But the centuries of Christian development have demonstrated that the antagonism between these two poles of what might be called Mediterranean humanity is not inexorable, perhaps even that the tensions between them are a necessary element in a particular view of the world that has become characteristic of Western civilization.

As has been argued throughout this book, modern man exists in a situation that brings about a much more comprehensive "ecumene" than was possible even in the cosmopolitan time of Tertullian. Today, the ecumene truly embraces mankind as a whole. In this new "ecumenicity," the relative proximity of Athens and Jerusalem becomes much more apparent. They are really not very far from each other, these two little towns that have played such a big role in the story of *Homo mediterraneus*. Other polarities become much more important now. As far as the religious history of mankind is concerned, none is more significant than the one between India and western Asia. And a quite different question now becomes prominent and pressing: *What is Benares to Jerusalem?* Much of the future course of religion hinges on the answer that will be given to *this* question.

"The Dharma Is Going West"

The panorama of man's religious quest at first appears to contain an almost endless array of different possibilities. Yet, upon closer scrutiny, these possibilities come to be ordered in terms of far fewer types. Once one passes from mere classification to an assessment of those possibilities that are truly "interesting," one almost inevitably comes to focus on the aforementioned polarity.[1] Put simply, western Asia and India have given birth to the two most comprehensive religious worldviews, and the antithesis between them constitutes the most important problem for contemporary ecumenicity. Now every historian of religion will immediately send up bright red warning flags upon hearing such a statement, and it is most advisable to heed these warnings. Nothing in human life can be understood in terms of clear-cut and generally applicable antitheses, and religion is no exception to this. The empirical reality of history is full of in-between colors and only rarely presents a picture of stark black-and-white contrasts. Thus, however one may want to typify the religious phenomena indigenous to western Asia and India respectively, the historian will be able to show how these types were only rarely found in pure form, how they intermingled and interpenetrated each other. All of this should be stipulated. But precisely because of all this intermingling, it is important to perceive just *what* it was that intermingled. Only then can the distinctiveness of the different religious possibilities be perceived at all. In other words, the history of religion is *not* a night in which all cats are gray.

Western Asia has been characterized by an experience of the divine as the personal God who speaks to man. To say that this is the religious experience of monotheism is to refer to only one aspect of the matter, for the oneness of the divine can be affirmed as a result of quite different experiences. An equally important aspect is the confrontational character of the experience. God is not found within man but confronts man from the outside in acts of address. This is why western Asia has been the arena of what Max Weber called "emissary prophecy" —from Zoroaster and the Israelite prophets to Jesus and Muhammad. Just as this God of address is not to be found within man, so he is not to be identified with the cosmos or with any part of its natural reality. The fundamental struggle between Yahwism and the nature cults of the ancient Near East bring this difference into sharp relief. The God of Israel was totally different from the divinities to be attained through the natural rhythms of the earth and of the human body, and this is why his spokesmen were so firm in their denunciations of the worship of fertility gods and of sacred sexuality. Yahweh was an "un-natural" divinity, in the literal sense of the word. Circumcision (whatever its origins may have been) became the most graphic expression in Israel of this scissure between faith in Yahweh and any form of "natural" religiosity. It is probable that Ahura Mazda, the divinity proclaimed by Zoroaster, had comparably "un-natural" traits. The later history of the religions emanating from this type of experience shows very clearly that maintaining the scissure was far from easy. Thus, again and again, the prophets of Israel had to denounce their compatriots for relapses into the old (and, one must assume, highly comforting) forms of nonconfrontational religiosity. But the distinctiveness of the Israelite religious experience becomes all the more clear in this ongoing struggle.

This God manifests himself as person, will, speech. To call this anthropomorphism is to miss the point; if anything, a term such as "anthropogenesis" would be more apt. For in the encounter with this God the conception of man becomes immeasurably sharpened. In this encounter *man* becomes profiled as person, will, speech. In other words, this particular religious experience is immeasurably individuating. One could also say that, in this encounter with God, man becomes lonely in the world (so that, in the most literal sense, the Israelite nostalgia for the old fertility cults was a yearning for the old company). Man becomes aware of himself *as man* in the encounter with the God who addresses him. This also entails a fundamental rupture between man and cosmos. The cosmos ceases to be divine in its own right, as it was (probably cross-culturally) in the millennia of early human history. Instead, the cosmos, as God's creation, becomes real in its own right. The cosmos is now perceived as the arena of God's action—and, by the same token, the arena of the acts of man (be these acts in response to or in defiance of God's address). In other words, this particular religious experience is both historicizing and moralizing. It is in the same religious experience (albeit in conjunction with the rather different Hellenic experiences of reason and human autonomy) that one must seek the specifically Western constellation of individual, history, and conscience.[2]

There is probably no clearer case of this root experience than the so-called throne vision of the prophet Isaiah (Isaiah 8). God reveals himself to Isaiah in this vision of unspeakable and terrifying grandeur. But this revelation, while overwhelming the prophet with a sense of God, at the same time changes his perception of himself—as a man of "unclean lips." Transcendence and conscience stand in a dialectical relation to each other in this experience. What is more, the import of this entire hierophany is precisely to accredit Isaiah as an emissary of God—to go out and proclaim God's message, a message that is full of history and full of morality. This individuating, historicizing, and moralizing effect of the Israelite experience of God has persisted through the centuries of Jewish and Christian history since Isaiah, and (albeit with some modifications) it is fundamental to Islam as well.[3]

If the religious experience distinctive to western Asia can be called confrontational, then that distinctive to India is marked by interiority. The divine does not confront man from the outside but is to be sought within himself as the divine ground of his own being and of the cosmos. The divine here is metapersonal and beyond all attributes, including those of will and speech. Once the divine ground of being is grasped, both man and cosmos pale into insignificance or even illusiveness. Individuality is not sharpened but absorbed, and both history and morality are radically relativized. Needless to say, there is an immense variety of expressions of these experiences in the rich history of Indian and Indian-derived religiosity, and this history also contains experiences that are much closer to the west-Asian prototype. The fundamental difference remains all the same.

From the earliest times of Indian history, religion has been marked by the practice of interiority and by the theory of *samsara-karma* (the wheel of reincarnations and the inexorable consequences of human acts over a sequence of reincarnations). It is possible, perhaps even likely, that these twin phenomena antedate the Aryan invasion of the subcontinent.[4] In the pre-Aryan ruins of the Indus civilization archaeologists have found statuettes of individuals in the postures of Yoga contemplation. If there is a protypical gestalt of Indian religiosity, it is surely the Yogin sitting in the lotus position—silent, withdrawn from the world, passive, turned inward in his quest of the ultimate reality within himself. This figure is central not only to Hinduism but also to the great heterodox religious movements of India, notably Jainism and Buddhism. And in its Buddhist version the same figure has been central to the religious experience of eastern Asia. It is difficult to conceive of a figure more antithetical to that of the Israelite prophet.

There is a Hindu legend about a meeting between a young saint (one who has attained knowledge of salvation, which means release from the wheel of *samsara*) and Indra, the great god of creation. The two are talking in Indra's heavenly palace when suddenly the saint laughs. "Why are you laughing?" asks Indra. "The ants, the ants," replies the saint, pointing to a trail of ants making their way across the marble floor of the palace.

And when Indra fails to understand, the saint explains: "Every one of these ants has been Indra—and will be Indra again." In this (to a Western mind, bloodcurdling) statement lies a whole universe of the Indian experience of reality—not only of the nature of the gods but of the world, of man, and of human events. Without this experience one cannot understand either the practice or the theory of Indian religion—from the day-to-day manifestations of the caste system to the grandiose speculations of both Hindu and Buddhist thought. Here indeed is the heart of Benares—at the opposite pole of human possibilities from what took place in and around Jerusalem.

Western Asia and India are part of the same continental land mass, and the two prototypes of religious experience and reflection did not develop without mutual contact. Sometimes the contact was quite massive. Some scholars believe that there were Indian influences on a number of the Greek mystery cults (which in turn influenced early Christianity). Gnosticism, which was a serious rival of Christianity over a period of several centuries, has been seen as a curious mixture of Hindu themes with Iranian dualism (Iran, for the most obvious reasons, has always been a bridge between the two poles). Probably the most intense contestation between the two prototypical forms of religion took place within Islam, particularly in the development of Muslim mysticism (and, again, particularly in Iran). However, for reasons elaborated early in this book, the modern situation provides an altogether novel context for contestation.

Originally, this context was brought about, above all, by the imperialistic push of Western (ipso facto Christian) civilization into Asia. Needless to say, this imperialism was based on political and economic rationales, not religious ones. All the same, it allowed not only for an aggressive missionary invasion of Asia by the major Christian churches (and in some places, such as China, the missionaries had some moderate successes), but much more importantly it was under the umbrella of Western imperialism that the forces of modernization were unleashed in all these countries. Modernity, even in its most secularized versions, is a product of Western Christian civilization, and it continues to evince its roots. Christianity as a religious faith did not make spectacular headway in Asia, but as the modernization process brought about an acculturation of, for example, Western notions of the individual, of history, or of social ethics in Asian countries, this too may be seen as a kind of contestation. Gandhi could not be imagined without this contestation. Neither could the dramatic modernization of Japan. But even in China in a paradoxical way indeed, the missionaries were finally successful: Marxism, after all, represents a secularized version of Christian eschatology. (The point that the old China missionaries would have been horrified by their "success" is immaterial: History is the long record of unintended consequences.) In any case, the original form of the contestation was the Christian West pushing itself forcefully into Asia.

Even then, in the heyday of triumphant Western imperialism, the relation was not one of unidirectional domination. Asia both puzzled and intrigued its Western invaders, and already in the eighteenth and early nineteenth centuries Asian mentality (including its religious aspects) had an influence on some Western thinkers. One may only mention Goethe, Schopenhauer, and Emerson in this connection. But the second half of the twentieth century is not only a postcolonial era in a political and economic sense. It is also postcolonial culturally, as the powerful upsurge of the so-called Third World demonstrates every day. The present contention is that the religious dimension of this postcolonialism is now beginning to become manifest.

Benares is taking its revenge. As Christian missionaries used to swarm into India and China, so Hindu and Buddhist missionaries are today roaming the streets of Western cities, in America above all. The eruption of Asian religiosity in America in the late 1960s was, of course, at least in part a matter of fashion and faddism. But it is safe to say that it was more than that. To be sure, some of the more flamboyant expressions of the "Age of Aquarius" have gone. Also, relatively small numbers of Americans are explicit adherents of Asian religious groups.[5] But much larger numbers are engaged in meditational practices of Asian provenance.[6] What is more difficult to measure is a heightened awareness of Asian visions of reality in segments of American culture. Anyone who peruses periodicals close to the ecology movement, for instance, or who observes the continuing interest in Asian religions on college campuses, is likely to conclude that this influence is much broader than one would guess from the numbers of those who directly identify themselves with Asian religiosity.

Within the small circles of Hinduism and Buddhism in America, not surprisingly, there are very wide expectations for this reversal of the missionary thrust. Thus Buddhists talk about "the dharma going west," and they see this as opening a new era in the history of Buddhism comparable in importance to the great movement of the dharma out of India into the countries of the Far East. A less involved observer is unlikely to agree with these expectations too quickly. Nothing in human history is impossible, but the conversion of substantial portions of the American people to Buddhism does not seem to be a probable scenario. Such predictions, however, are not presupposed in the present proposition that a new contestation between Jerusalem and Benares is in the making. For this proposition to be valid, it is not necessary that American Buddhists rival Methodists or Presbyterians in the denominational statis-

tics. Rather, it is the sheer presence of Buddhism in the
religious consciousness of America that is relevant. What *can*
be predicted is that this presence will not go away. It will have
to be dealt with intellectually. What is so with regard to Buddhism is also so with the Benares prototype in a wider sense.

It is interesting to observe how few Christian theologians
show any interest in the non-Western religions. Most Christian
theology today, be it Protestant or Catholic, liberal or conservative, goes on as if the Judaeo-Christian tradition were alone
in the world—with modern secularity as its only external conversation partner. There are exceptions. Both the Vatican
(through its Secretariat for the Non-Christian Religions) and
the World Council of Churches have been carrying on a program of dialogue with representatives of Asian religions. Harvey Cox and Robert Bellah have given thoughtful attention
recently to the Asian religious presence in America.[7] Raymond
Panikkar and John Hick have made very serious efforts to
reformulate some aspects of Christian doctrine by confronting
it with Indian religiosity.[8] There are some other interesting
efforts in the same direction.[9] It is still fair to say that the
contestation is as yet in a virtually embryonic phase.

The present proposition is not simply that Christian theologians should pay attention to Asia. The question is *what kind*
of attention is to be paid. Thus what is meant here by contestation is *not* attention by means of detached scholarship. *Nor* is
it the sort of dialogue that could be described as reciprocal an-
tidefamation—one religious tradition explaining itself to
others, with the aim of increasing mutual understanding and
tolerance. Both of these two kinds of attention are certainly
valid, even praiseworthy, but they are not contestation in the
present sense. Needless to say, what is intended here is also *not*
attention paid to another religious tradition in order to evan-

gelize its adherents more effectively—the discipline that used to be called *Missionswissenschaft* and that is happily on the wane today. *Contestation means an open-minded encounter with other religious possibilities on the level of their truth claims.* Put differently, one seriously engages another religion if one is open, at least hypothetically, to the proposition that this other religion is true. Put differently again, to enter into interreligious contestation is to be prepared to change one's own view of reality. Anything short of this, however valuable it may be (for scholarship, say, or for joint sociopolitical concerns, or just for an enlargement of cultural horizons), is less than the contestation called for by the present situation. It is *this* kind of contestation that is as yet in an embryonic phase.

Now it is important that one particular misunderstanding be avoided here: To say that Jerusalem and Benares are heading for a new contestation is *not* to predict the outcome of this contestation. It is certainly *not* to predict, or to hope for, any kind of grand synthesis. Such a synthesis, if it were possible at all (there have been a few attempts in the past), would almost certainly be a pale, abstract construction, an intellectual artifact in which streams of living religious experience would be reduced to their least common denominator. If that were the outcome, it would be better if no contestation took place. The above definition of contestation implies the readiness to say yes to the truth claims of another religious tradition; equally important is the readiness, in principle, to say no. *To consider the truth claims of the Indian vision of the world is not to assent to it a priori.* Indeed, anyone starting on this contestation from a Christian or Jewish point of departure will expect to end up saying no on a number of issues. But, by the same token, it is unlikely that such an individual, if he is truly open-minded, will end up saying no on *all* issues. Even one yes, however, would mean a modification of the Judaeo-Christian vision. In other words, *once this contestation is entered, it is unlikely that its participants will remain unchanged.*

The Divine in Confrontation and Interiority

One might now state the character of the polarity a little more sharply (and at the same time in a manner that would make historians of religion less nervous): There are two distinct types of religious experience characterized, respectively, by *confrontation with the divine* and by the *interiority of the divine.* To say this is to propose ideal types in a Weberian sense: That is, the two types do not necessarily exist in pure form empirically; they interpenetrate, and there are mixed or compromise versions. Now, while both types of religious experience may be found cross-culturally, they are not distributed equally across the spectrum of human cultures. Thus western Asia has been characterized by a strong concentration of the first type, India and the religious cultures influenced by India by a strong concentration of the second type. If one looks at the matter in this somewhat more careful way, then the two poles of Jerusalem and Benares are not absolute opposites, but rather appear as poles in an almost statistical sense: They are, as it were, the centers of two clusters of religious experience. This more cautious way of formulating the antithesis, however, in no way detracts from its importance. Thus most historians would agree that the three great monotheistic religions coming out of the biblical experience have a strong, built-in bias against mysticism (which is the characteristic par excellence of the interiority type). Indeed, in ancient Israel as well as in Zoroastrian Iran it is virtually impossible to find *any* manifestations of mysticism (unless one wants to call sacred sexuality an archaic form of mystical experience). By contrast, India throughout its history has been extremely hospitable to mysticism, to the point that one historian has aptly called India "the high school of mysticism."[10]

In the aforementioned contestations between the Jerusalem and Benares types in earlier periods of history, not surprisingly, it was the relation between confrontation and interiority that posed an urgent problem of interpretation. From the standpoint of Jerusalem, the problem is formulated as follows: *If God revealed himself in the Torah (or, of course, in Jesus Christ, or in the Koran), how could he also be found within the interiority of mystical consciousness?* From the standpoint of Benares, the inverse formulation pertains: *If the divine is to be experienced as the true ground of every man's consciousness, what is the status of particular historical revelations?*

The sociology of knowledge provides a useful perspective on precisely such situations of cognitive conflict, and a category deriving from that discipline is useful here—that of nihilation. One speaks of nihilation when one cognitive system develops ways of interpreting the truth claims of a rival cognitive system as being null and void, thus neutralizing the implicit threat to its own truth claims. Both Jerusalem and Benares are fully capable of thus nihilating each other. The claims of the mystics have been interpreted over and over again as idolatry, illusion, or gifts of the devil by the upholders of Jewish, Christian, and Muslim orthodoxy. The Barthian rejection of every conceivable form of mysticism as "unbelief" is only a recent expression of this venerable tradition of anathematization. This attitude is, of course, particularly congenial to religious groups carrying on aggressive missionary activities. But one should not be misled by the proverbial tolerance of Benares. There is a peculiarly Hindu and Buddhist form of nihilation as well. It typically proceeds by interpreting the experiences of the confrontational type as being of an inferior religious status, at worst expressing a state of spiritual benightedness, at best being useful stages toward a higher form of experience in which they are destined to be dissolved. In this perspective, the personalistic piety of a Jew or a Muslim is childish make-believe when compared with true enlightenment. If this is tolerance, it is of a very patronizing sort.

There is a more promising way of approaching the problem. It becomes possible if one accepts the methodological presuppositions of the inductive approach proposed here—especially the presupposition that all of human religious experience must be taken with utmost seriousness. In this perspective it seems highly improbable, to say the least, that the millennia of Hindu and Buddhist experience can be subsumed under the heading of idolatry or illusion. Conversely, it seems most implausible to look upon the prophet Isaiah as an infantile intimation of what every ordinary Tibetan monk takes for granted. But if the truth claims of neither confrontation nor interiority are nihilated in such fashion, a much more interesting question can be formulated: *How could it be possible that both types of religious experience are true?*

Let this be contended, then: If there is to be a new contestation between Jerusalem and Benares, this last question is a pretty good one to start off the agenda. Luckily, in view of the awesome complexity of the question, others have asked it before. A pretty good *modus operandi* would be a new look at earlier attempts to give an answer. Now, as mentioned before, the two types of religious experience have not been in a pure or absolute opposition to each other historically; rather they have interpenetrated. There is a rich history of mystical movements in the three great monotheistic traditions; there are powerful eruptions of confrontational piety in Hinduism and Buddhism. Put schematically, there are Benares-type phenomena within the Jerusalem matrix, and Jerusalem-type phenomena within the Benares matrix. These cases obviously posed a cognitive problem. The guardians of the official traditions of either type could always deal with the problem by simple nihilation, and very often they did just that (and often enough they went in from the theoretical voiding of the heresy to the practical liquidation of the heretic). Those who deviated from the traditions did not have this easy way out: They had to explain themselves. The cognitive strategies employed by these individuals are of very great usefulness in an approach to the problem. Also luckily, some of them were thinkers of great force and originality.

Mysticism too is not a monolithic phenomenon, and its manifestations within either the Jerusalem or the Benares matrix show a considerable variety.[11] If mysticism is defined in the broad way suggested before—that is, as a religious quest turned inward, seeking the divine within the interiority of human consciousness—then one may even find mystical elements in Luther's otherwise highly confrontational piety, and certainly in such inward-looking forms of religion as Methodism (Wesley's "warmed heart") and the revivalistic consciousness-alterations of much of American Protestantism. On the contemporary scene, even the charismatic movement may be said to be more mystical than the sober confrontation with "Word and Sacrament" of orthodox Christian piety. Such forms of quasi mysticism have posed problems for the official guardians of the traditions, if only because of their emotionalism and their frequent disrespect for ecclesiastical authorities, but the cognitive threat posed by them has been relatively mild. All of them can be subsumed under the heading of what some scholars have called the "mysticism of personality," meaning by that forms of inward experience in which, despite the intensity such experience may sometimes reach, there is no dissolution of the

human personality nor a forgetting of the personal and transcendent character of God. The much more serious cognitive
threat has come from another kind of mystical experience, the
one often called the "mysticism of infinity" by scholars, in
which the individual believes himself to completely lose his
own personal qualities and to merge into union with the divine, whether directly within his own consciousness or through
an experience of unity with the natural universe. It can be said
very safely that this type of mysticism has always been at home
within the Benares matrix, and the worldviews of both Hinduism and Buddhism have always been very hospitable to it.
One may also say that the classical interpretation of this experience is to be found in the Upanishads, especially in the
Upanishadic idea of the ultimate unity of the deepest reality of
the human soul (Atman) and the divine essence of the universe (Brahman). The famous Upanishadic formula "you are
that" (tat tvam asi) refers to this unity, grasping which in
mystical experience is the goal of the salvific quest. This same
idea, of course, has received enormously sophisticated elaborations in Indian philosophy, especially in the monistic
(Advaita) school of the Vedanta.[12] While the interpretations of this experience are quite different in Buddhist
thought (and, for that matter, in Jainism and in the Samkhya
theory of Yoga), there too the experience poses no cognitive
threat to the overall religious worldview.

Eruptions of such "mysticism of infinity" have had a very
different effect within the matrix of the monotheistic religions
of western Asia. In the latter matrix such experiences immediately put in question the revelation of the personal and transcendent God embodied in the tradition—the God of Abraham, Isaac, and Jacob, who gave the Torah to Moses; the
Father of Our Lord Jesus Christ; the God who revealed the
Koran to Muhammad, the God who has no companions or as-

sociates. One of the most central characteristics of this God is his utter otherness with regard to man, whom he confronts in absolute and awesome majesty (as in the throne vision of Isaiah). To suggest, as the "mysticism of infinity" does, that man can experience unity with *this* God is to raise right away the suggestion of blasphemy. Not surprisingly then, Jewish, Christian, and Muslim religious authorities have often reacted vehemently against mystics of this type, the reaction sometimes going as far as bloody persecution. A classical case of this is the fate of the Muslim mystic al-Hallaj, who was executed in Baghdad in 922 for reiterating the formula "I am truth" (*ana'l-haqq*), a formula which the authorities understood (probably correctly) as implying identification with God.[13]

Those who contend that mystical experience is the same throughout the world, or that this cross-cultural mysticism is the true foundation of all religion, usually have the "mysticism of infinity" in mind; the other kind, the "mysticism of personality," is too obviously variegated to suggest such ideas. The notion that this variety of religious experience is the true foundation of all religion is a declaration of faith, which has little if any support in the empirical evidence. But the proposition that the "mysticism of infinity" is always the same, despite variations in interpretation, is very powerfully supported by the evidence. William James put this very clearly: "The fact is that the mystical feeling of enlargement, union and emancipation has no specific intellectual content whatever of its own. It is capable of forming matrimonial alliances with material furnished by the most diverse philosophies and theologies, provided only they can find a place in their framework for its peculiar emotional mood."[14] There is here also, of course, the methodological presupposition that the experiential core of this kind of mysticism can be unraveled from the "matrimonial alliances" with this or that kind of theorizing about it. And one may add, in line with the foregoing, that the accommodation of the experience within the prevailing theoretical "framework" has always been much easier in Benares than in Jerusalem.

A dramatic demonstration of the similarity of this kind of mystical experience was made by Rudolf Otto, in his comparative study of the medieval mystic Meister Eckhart and the great Vedanta teacher Shankara.[15] Eckhart lived in Germany from 1250 to 1327, Shankara in India around 800. It is very hard to imagine how the writings of the latter could have influenced the former, yet repeatedly, as Otto points out, the words of one "read like a translation into Latin or German from the Sanskrit of the other, and vice versa."[16] It followed for Otto that the two were both attempting to articulate the same experience. It is a reasonable conclusion. After all, a German-speaking person of the High Middle Ages describing a sunset would, in all probability, come up with formulations very similar to those of an individual of ninth-century India describing a sunset in Sanskrit. It would then be reasonable to conclude that both individuals did in fact watch sunsets, and it would be unnecessary to hypothetize that one somehow copied from the other (by whatever route of successive plagiarisms). But there is a difference of course: It is pretty clear what a sunset is; the same, alas, cannot be said of mystical experience. Consequently, even if one allows that there is a universal experience underlying all the different accounts, one must still ask just what this experience really is. Many of the mystics themselves asked the very same question. Eckhart did; so did Shankara.

Much more interesting than the fact that both Eckhart and Shankara apparently had the same experience is the fact that this experience drove them to amazingly similar interpretations. The theoretical matrix within which Shankara was working (essentially the "framework" provided by the Upanishads) made this relatively easy. Shankara too had to give an account of other types of religious experience—to wit, the Hindu versions of the confrontational experience, in the encounter with a variety of personal gods and in the personal devotion (*bhakti*) to these gods. One may even say (as Otto did) that there was a "theistic foundation" to Shankara's speculation, given by his notion of the supreme god Ishvara, comparable to the God of the biblical tradition. The question then becomes how the Brahman, the ultimate reality with which the human soul experiences union and identity, relates to Ishvara. There can be no doubt that, for Shankara, any encounter with Ishvara is but an inferior step on the road to the Brahman. Indeed, as the Brahman is not only the ultimate but the only true reality, Ishvara is finally seen to be an illusion (*maya*)—a religiously useful illusion, perhaps (useful, that is, for those who have not yet progressed to the higher levels of understanding), but an illusion all the same. The gods (including Ishvara) come and go. They issue out of the Brahman and return to it again. In the end, only the Brahman remains. And the Brahman is beyond all qualities, including the quality of personhood. As the individual soul merges with the Brahman, as a drop of water dissolves in the ocean, it too passes beyond the illusion of the gods and personal piety (even devotion to Ishvara) becomes meaningless.

The theoretical matrix of medieval Catholicism was not so hospitable to formulations of this sort. Yet Eckhart produced very similar ones, apparently compelled to do so by the very force of his own experience. The central place of this in his writings is the conceptualization of the relation of God and "Godhead." God, of course, is the biblical God, the God of Christian piety in the orthodox manner. Godhead is the divine that transcends this God. Like the Brahman, it is metapersonal and beyond all qualities. And, like Shankara, Eckhart teaches

that at the heights of mystical experience the soul attains unity
with Godhead—and thus passes beyond all intercourse with
God. Indeed, there are passages in which Eckhart speaks of
God becoming and disbecoming, coming out of the Godhead
and dissolving within it. Such formulations are clearly in sharp
contradiction to the ultimacy of the biblical God, as experienced in confrontation with him. It is only natural that these
and similar formulations of Eckhart's were condemned by the
church (luckily after his death).

Ecclesiastical condemnations rarely end such matters. The
"mysticism of infinity" continued to plague Catholic orthodoxy
—right after Eckhart by his almost as daring disciple Suso, and
by other Catholic mystics ever since. Even Protestantism produced mystics such as Jacob Boehme and Angelus Silesius, who
also came forth with appallingly Hindu-sounding statements.
The entire history of Jewish mysticism is full of similar
conflicts, and the great mystical thinkers in Judaism (such as
Isaac Luria) produced similarly daring formulations on the
relation between the infinite (en-sof) of the mystical experience and the embarrassingly personal God of the Covenant. It
is probably the Islamic case—that is, the case of the problems
of Sufi mysticism within its Islamic context—which is the most
instructive one. Perhaps this is because Islam is the only world
religion that physically spanned the distance from Benares to
Jerusalem. The extent to which Sufism was directly influenced
by Hindu practices and ideas is in dispute among scholars.[17] Be
this as it may, the conflict between the confrontational and the
interiorized types of religious experience was carried on in the
Islamic context with particular intensity—and also, to the
benefit of later students of the matter, with particular sophistication. Indeed, if it was argued earlier in this book that Protestantism constitutes the paradigmatic case of the encounter
between religion and modernity, one might argue that Islam

constitutes a comparably paradigmatic case of the encounter between Jerusalem and Benares.

The details of this, obviously, cannot be elaborated here. A key concept in this area is the Sufi one of *fana*, which denotes the fading away or dissolution of the self in the throes of mystical experience. There can be little doubt that this refers to the same experience that the "mystics of infinity" report from widely divergent parts of the world. And a number of Sufi mystics interpreted this experience in a manner that suggests the ultimate identity of the self with the divine and that employs language that Shankara and Eckhart would have found congenial. Reference has already been made to al-Hallaj. There were others. A particularly fascinating case is that of Abu Yazid of Bistam, who at times uses language that seems a direct translation of Hindu texts, as in the following passage (which may even contain the classical Upanishadic formula "you are that!"): "Once God raised me up and placed me before him, and said to me: 'O Abu Yazid, verily my creation longs to see thee.' And I said: 'Adorn me with thy unity and clothe me in thine I-ness and raise me up unto thy oneness, so that when thy creatures see me, they may say: 'We have seen thee [i.e., God] and *thou art that*.' Yet I [Abu Yazid] will not be there at all."[18]

Abu Yazid, although he (just like al-Hallaj) continued to proclaim himself a Muslim, seems not to have recoiled from the pantheistic consequences of such formulations. Others did, and tried to interpret the experience of *fana* in a manner more compatible with orthodox Islam. Qushayri developed an extremely sophisticated psychological theory of mystical experience, in which it is argued that the mystic undergoes cycles of "expansion" and "contraction" in his experience, and that the more extravagant formulations can be traced to the distortions in perception brought about by the expansive phase. Junayd, in

his commentary on Abu Yazid, maintained that the experience
of *fana*, in which the mystic believes himself to be one with
God (also called the *mir'aj*, or "ascension"), is only one of several stages on the mystic path—the final stage is *not* one of
unity with God but one of loving adoration (which, in the
terms used here, would have to be called confrontational).
And al-Ghazali, the great philosopher who was more responsi-
ble than anyone for making Sufism a respectable part of the
divine sciences in Islam, was inconsistent on the matter, though
he also (like Qushayri) played down the excessive claims to
unity with the divine by means of psychological explanation.[19]

If the "mysticism of infinity" has created cognitive problems
for the traditions of the Jerusalem matrix, so manifestations of
confrontational piety have done so within Hinduism and Buddhism. In the Hindu case, of course, there has always been a
rich tradition of personal devotion (*bhakti*) to particular
divinities, notably Vishnu and Shiva. The Bhagavad Gita has
been taken as a guidebook for just this kind of devotion,
though it also contains elements of the other type of religious
experience. A fascinating figure of what may be called "confrontational Hinduism" is Ramanuja, the twelfth-century philosopher, who is particularly interesting because he explicitly
criticized Shankara and his disciples.[20] For Ramanuja, the
highest experience of the divine is in the face-to-face confrontation of loving devotion. The experiences of unity and of ab-
sorption into an impersonal divinity are imperfect stages on the
path to this highest experience. Ramanuja criticized Shankara
precisely because the latter stopped at this lower point on the
journey toward God, calling it the highest point. According to
Ramanuja, what the mystic experiences at this lower point is
indeed real—it is the essential nature of his own self and that
of the universe—but it is not yet God. In this, Ramanuja's formulations are strikingly similar to those of Junayd and some of

the Christian mystics who were careful to stop short of an interpretation of their experience that would invalidate biblical
theism. In the Buddhist case, very likely, the best examples of
similar cognitive problems will come from the Mahayana. Reference has already been made to the case of the Pure Land
school of Japan, with its quasi-"Lutheran" devotion to the sav-
ior figure of Amida. The cognitive problem here is how such
personalistic and confrontational piety is to be reconciled with
a metaphysic in which the self is finally understood to be an illusion (an-atta) and in which the fundamental category of the
universe is understood as emptiness (shunyata). But none of
these lines of investigation can be pursued here any further.

In sum, leaving aside the cruder mutual interpretations of
those upholding the experiences of confrontation and interiority (illusion on the one hand, illusion and/or idolatry on
the other), there have also been mutual interpretations that do
not invalidate the "other party." One of the fullest discussions
of these may be found in a work by R. C. Zaehner,[21] who, as a
Roman Catholic, was very open about his own bias: He clearly
took the side of Ramanuja against Shankara, and of Junayd
against Abu Yazid. Yet he was fair to the other side. He spells
out the manner in which a Shankara might characterize the
personal devotion of, say, a Christian believer in Christ. Any
personal God, in this perspective, is what the Hindus call (in
mind-boggling anticipation of American religious pluralism!) a
"deity of one's preference" (ishta-devata). As such, Christ is an
"adjunct" (upadhi) for the religious believer, a focus of devotion (one might even say a "handle") by means of which individuals with a certain background may actually make religious
progress. In the final experience of the Brahman, all these "ad-
juncts" will be revealed to be of a lesser reality. This need not
mean that they are relegated to a status of utter nonbeing.

Still, there will be no question but that standard Christian piety is religion of a lesser rank.

Conversely, it is not necessary for the Christian (or the Jew, the Muslim or the practitioner of Hindu *bhakti*) to repudiate the experiences of the "mysticism of infinity." These experiences may be understood as stages on the way to the beatific vision of the personal and transcendent God, an emptying of the mind to facilitate the next stages of the journey. Zaehner quotes the Flemish Christian mystic Ruysbroeck to good effect here. Ruysbroeck accepted the experience of mystic emptiness (what Buddhists call *shunyata*), but only in conjunction with other elements of the Christian life. He condemned the experience when it is taken as an end in itself, and particularly when it is divorced from the moral demands of the Christian life, for this experience can be found by "all men, however evil they may be, if they live in their sins with untroubled conscience, and are able to empty themselves of all images and all action."[22] One is reminded here of William James's insistence that the final test of religious experience (mystical or other) must be moral—"by their fruits you shall know them." There are difficulties with this position: What is one to do with the fact that seemingly identical experiences are reported by individuals whom one would readily call saintly (say, Teresa of Avila) and individuals whose lives were morally reprehensible in the extreme? (A good example of the later possibility would be the sinister Brother Joseph, emissary of Cardinal Richelieu, who among other things encouraged the unspeakable horrors of the Thirty Years' War in Germany—and who was a practitioner or unceasing mystical prayer!) Be this as it may, Zaehner sums up this way of interpreting the "mysticism of infinity" from a Christian standpoint: "Delectable though this state obviously it will, be filled with God. *Emptiness is the prelude to Holi-* with God; it is only the purification of the vessel which can, if it will, be filled with God. *Emptiness is the prelude to Holiness.*[23]

The contestation between Jerusalem and Benares has not reached the point where one would too quickly assent to any of these formulations. There is much work to be done in exploring earlier attempts to deal cognitively with the discrepant experiences at issue. And out of this may come altogether new cognitive possibilities. One thing, though, should be clear: Here are crucial problems for an inductive approach to religion. They should have high priority on an agenda for a Christian theology using inductive methods.[24]

While Waiting for the Dark Drums of God

Throughout this book the effort has been made to develop an argument that can be followed by reasonable men from any religious background or standpoint. If theology is understood as reflection on the basis of faith and within a framework given by faith, then the argument of this book has been pretheological. (The definition of theology, of course, is arguable, but this is hardly the place to argue it.) Be this as it may, none of the foregoing was based on a Christian faith commitment (at least not intentionally). In conclusion, however, it may be appropriate to give up this, as it were, theoretical asceticism and to make some observations from an explicitly Christian standpoint.

What this does *not* mean should be clear from the preceding chapter: It does *not* mean to take one's stand on the basis of a "leap of faith," on some rock of immunity against rational and empirical criticism. *Even less* does it mean to succumb anew to the authority of Christian tradition, be it expressed in Scripture or in an ecclesiastical institution. What it *does* mean is quite simply this: the conviction that the core contents of the Christian message provide the fullest and most adequate interpretation of one's own experience of God, world, and self. Put differently, Christian faith here means to express the conviction that the universe ultimately makes sense in the light of Sinai and Calvary. It also means, if one wills, to take one's final stand in Jerusalem. Such a stand, needless to say, is not simply the taking of an intellectual position, of a particular theoretical approach. Rather, it involves the person as a whole, is "existential" in this simple sense. Perhaps enough has been said throughout this book to allay the suspicion that such a faith commitment must entail irrationalism, authoritarianism, or intolerance toward other views of the world. Whatever may be the weaknesses of the foregoing argumentation, fanaticism is hardly one of them.

It should be clearly stated, then, that the inductive method that has been proposed here for any systematic reflection about the religious phenomenon is *also* being proposed for explicitly Christian theology. It goes without saying that this presupposes a continuity between Christian theology and the general human enterprise of understanding the world rationally, including the rational undertakings of philosophy and the empirical sciences. This continuity, of course, is denied by the prevailing versions of neo-orthodoxy. In reaffirming it, one *ipso facto* repudiates neo-orthodoxy and places oneself in the line of liberal theology. One returns to Schleiermacher at least to the extent of assenting to his basic methodological program. By the same token, one considers both the neo-orthodox and the secularist movements in twentieth-century theology as aberrations to be laid aside.

It should also be clear that this does not imply a return to specific contents or themes of the older liberal theology. Some of these have been rendered obsolete by new scholarly insights;

others have lost plausibility as their sociocultural roots have become manifest. It is, of course, rarely if ever possible simply to return to an earlier intellectual position, and it is probably never desirable. But there is a more important reason why the agenda for Christian theology today should not be the same as the agenda that seemed obvious prior to the Barthian revolution: *The old agenda of liberal theology was the contestation with modernity. That agenda has exhausted itself. The much more pressing agenda today is the contestation with the fullness of human religious possiblities.*

So much of contemporary Christian theology still revolves around the question "What does modern man have to say to Christian faith?" The answers may be given in terms of this or that component of modern *Weltanschauung*, or of this or that modern cultural or sociopolitical praxis. To be sure, there are always things to be learned theoretically and practically from the new constellations brought forth by one's moment in history. Nothing said here is intended to recommend reactionary nostalgias or blindness to the new insights of twentieth-century life. Yet if anything impresses one today, it is the poverty of modernity. "What does modern man have to say to Christian faith?" The probable answer is: "Not much more than he has said already!" This fact accounts for the sterility of so much of what passes today for a Christian struggle with the *Zeitgeist* – the umpteenth reinterpretation of Hegel, Marx, or Freud so as to bring them into some sort of consonance with Christianity, or the umpteenth attempt to construct a plausible Christian praxis in the garb of this or that modern revolutionary movement—not to mention the anxious listening for the redeeming word in the latest outpourings of the sorry types proclaimed as culture prophets by the mass media. Most sterile of all is any renewed effort to make Christianity palatable to what is deemed to be the secular consciousness

of modern man. Such an effort is ironically futile in that
precisely this modern secularity is in crisis today. The most
obvious fact about the contemporary world is not so much its
secularity, but rather its great hunger for redemption and for
transcendence.

In this situation Christian theology needs first of all a *prise
de conscience* of its own heritage, something that presupposes
critical distance to the cacophony of contemporary culture and
to the assumptions of modern secularity. It means a *prise de
conscience*—indeed, a *reprise*—of the religious phenomenon as
such and of its Christian variant. In no way need this entail the
reconstructionist turn of neo-orthodoxy or neotraditionalism in
any form. In the final analysis, it means a *reprise*, a reappropria-
tion, of one's own experience. It also means an attitude of faithfulness to one's own experience. The same attitude will then determine how one deals with whatever tradition one may find in
one's biographical and social background. But the present contention is that this is not enough—at least not enough for
those who want to meet the cognitive challenges of the present
situation. For them, to repeat, the contestation with the
religious alternatives to Christian faith should stand high on
the list of intellectual priorities.

The last thing in the world that this intends to suggest is
that comparative religion should now take the place of history,
psychology, sociology, or whatever other modern disciplines
have been used to translate theology into. Far from it: Comparative religion, as an empirical discipline, can only supply certain data, which can then become part of the contestation. As
soon as one engages oneself with the truth claims of a tradition, one has left the domain of comparative religion. There is
no need to repeat the preceding arguments for the proposition
that such interreligious contestation should be an urgent concern for anyone reflecting about religious matters today. But it

is noteworthy that advances in Christian theology have typically occurred through contestations (in this, probably, theology is no different from other intellectual enterprises): What is "one's own" becomes clear in confrontation with an "other."

Let it be stipulated, as generously as one wills, that modernity, and even modern secularity, has been such an "other" for a few centuries. Let the cognitive gains of this contestation be gratefully acknowledged—and, from here on in, taken for granted! This acknowledgment and taken-for-granted appropriation should certainly include the modern disciplines of history and the social sciences. Having expressed one's appreciation, one can then go on to other things. To be sure, there continue to be individuals to whom these cognitive gifts of modernity are still startling, disturbing, enormously provocative. Typically these are individuals who have just emerged from this or that narrow religious milieu and for whom modernity is a great emancipation. One may applaud their liberation and heartily concur in their discovery that the modern situation is to be preferred (at least intellectually) to the underworld of their upbringing. But there is no reason why one should share their awe of modernity or why their discovery that they are or have become modern men should become a permanent theological agenda. One may say then, as has been done here, that a different "other" than modernity may be a more fruitful stimulant for Christian theology. This "other," to repeat, is the incredibly rich panorama of world religions—immensely more promising for the Christian theologian as it is immensely more fruitful to delve into the Upanishads than into the latest products of contemporary ideologists. In sum, *to turn from the contestation with modernity to the contestation with Benares is to break through the impasse of contemporary Christian theology.*

This chapter has been subtitled, rather optimistically, "The

Coming Contestation of Religions." This optimism should perhaps be qualified. The subtitle is not intended as a sociological
prediction. On the level of sociocultural reality, of course, the
contestation is already taking place. That contestation is, as has
been argued, of the essence of the pluralistic situation. But will
this situation be taken up as a challenge by Christian theology?
Or, for that matter, by thinkers in other religious traditions? It
would be foolhardy to make predictions on this. History is full
of cases where the challenges of a situation were missed or mis-
understood. The contestation in question *should* come—that is
one proposition; the other is that, if it comes, it will occasion a
revitalization of religious thought in whatever tradition partici-
pates in it.

For Christian theology, such an inductive program will entail
a number of undertakings, which may well take place concur-
rently. There is, first of all, the ongoing *reprise* of the Christian
tradition itself, in the ongoing attempt to uncover the experiential substrata of the tradition and their "correlation" (to use
Tillich's happy term) with one's own experience. There is the
contestation with Judaism, so close at hand and yet so little engaged in by Christian theologians on its own cognitive as well
as experiential ground; despite the multifold Christian-Jewish
contacts, especially in America, it may safely be said that most
of these contacts (for various reasons) barely touch on questions of truth claims. There is the contestation with Islam, a
crucial alternative within the monotheistic orbit and a centrally
important bridge to the religious worlds of India. There is then
the great contestation with Benares that has been outlined in
this chapter. And let it also be said that nothing said here
about the contestation with the so-called world religions is intended to denigrate or to rule out the insights that may be
derived from religious traditions that have had lesser historical
scope—whether in Africa, the Americas, or elsewhere. No one

who has seen, for example, the temples of Tikal, rising magically out of the Guatemalan jungle, or has heard the drums of an African night, will wish to rule out of consideration the religious experiences represented by these manifestations.

Are there risks for Christian theology in such a program? There certainly are. But they are almost certainly no greater than the risks taken in earlier contestations—say, that with Greek philosophy in the patristic age and once again in medieval scholasticism, or in the application of modern historical scholarship to the Bible in the nineteeth century. Faithfulness to one's own experience has a personal as well as an intellectual dimension, as Troeltsch has expressed eloquently. This includes the mellow conviction that truth is always its own warrant and that, consequently, that which has imposed itself as truth by its own force will not be voided by subsequent discoveries of truth. If such an inductive program for theology should "fail," it will not be in the sense of a failure of faith. Intellectually, all programs "fail" in the end. There is no all-comprehensive, final, unshakable system of thought—not "in this aeon." To suggest a program for theology is not to hope for a final grand synthesis that will convince everybody. It is simply to suggest that a particular course of inquiries will be fruitful in this particular moment of history—no more, but also no less.

Another thing ought to be said again at this point: Religion is not, in its essence, an intellectual enterprise. Theologians are apt to forget this from time to time (in this they are no worse than other theorizing intellectuals). The history of Christianity is not the history of Christian theology. Rather, it is the history of a particular kind of religious experience and religious faith. Consequently, the future of Christianity will not depend on any theological program. One must be very careful, then, to resist the temptation to present one's own theological program as the one thing that will save the faith or the church in this

time. Such claims are always spurious (they are, incidentally, made with regularity all across the theological spectrum
from right to left). If Christianity has a future, it will be in the
resurgence of Christian experience and faith in the lives of people who have never read a theological book. Yet what the theologians do is not irrelevant to the unfolding of Christianity in
history. It can hinder or help. At times it can even play an important role (somebody once described the Lutheran Reformation as beginning with a conspiracy of junior faculty!). To suggest a particular theological program, then, is also to suggest
that theologians should be more helpful—again no more, but
also no less.

For the Christian, history is in the hands of God. The New
Testament tells Christians to be attentive to the signs of the
times, but it also suggests that the signs are hard to read and
that some may be misleading. The Lord is coming—that much
is affirmed in the trembling certainty of faith—but God will
decide on the when and how. Until the Lord comes, Christians
can only wait and meet the demands of the moment. This includes the intellectual demands. The religious thinker and the
theologian must also do what their situation demands of them,
but, as Christians, they must put aside excessive speculation as
to the outcome of their efforts. The signs of the present situation are also hard to read, confusing, and full of contradictory
possibilities—even in terms of sociological prediction, let alone
in terms of some eschatological scheme of history. The debate
over secularization is a good example of this. Historians and social scientists find it hard to agree on what secularization has
been in the past and on what it is today—let alone on what its
future course will be. The same goes for every other manifestation of modernity.

It is possible that a hundred years from now, say, modernity
will be pretty much what it is today. That would mean that

modern secularity will have overcome its present difficulties. It is also possible that the crisis of modernity will give birth to a powerful resurgence of religious forces, Christian or non-Christian. There is no reason to exclude the possibility that the future holds new, as yet inconceivable hierophanies. The Christian, and especially the Christian thinker, must remain open to all the possibilities of a future that lies in God's hands. In this attitude of openness, he must also try to meet the demands of the present moment.

There are times in history when the dark drums of God can barely be heard amid the noises of this world. Then it is only in moments of silence, which are rare and brief, that their beat can be faintly discerned. There are other times. These are the times when God is heard in rolling thunder, when the earth trembles and the treetops bend under the force of his voice. It is not given to men to make God speak. It is only given to them to live and to think in such a way that, if God's thunder should come, they will not have stopped their ears.

Notes

CHAPTER 1

1. Marion Levy, *Modernization: Latecomers and Survivors* (New York: Basic Books, 1972), p. 3.

2. My approach to this relation is that of the sociology of knowledge. The full implications of this approach obviously cannot be developed here. For the general theoretical underpinnings of the approach, see Peter L. Berger and Thomas Luckmann, *The Social Construction of Reality: A Treatise in The Sociology of Knowledge* (Garden City, N.Y.: Doubleday, 1966). For an application of the approach to the problem of modernity, sec Peter L. Berger, Brigitte Berger, and Hansfried Kellner, *The Homeless Mind: Modernization and Consciousness* (New York: Random House, 1973). The latter book in particular provides the overall theoretical framework for the present argument.

3. This understanding of the meaning of situatedness (*Standortsgebundenheit*) follows what has been called the moderate or less radical tradition in the sociology of knowledge, as against its more radically deterministic forms. See Werner Stark, *The Sociology of Knowledge* (Glencoe, Ill.: Free Press, 1958).

4. In *The Homeless Mind* we called these two sets of elements intrinsic and extrinsic ones, respectively.

5. Cf. William Greene, *Moira: Fate, Good and Evil in Greek Thought* (New York: Harper Torchbooks, 1963).

6. This understanding of legitimation provides the nexus between the sociologies of knowledge and religion. See my *The Sacred Canopy: Elements of a Sociological Theory of Religion* (Garden City, N.Y.: Doubleday, 1967). My understanding of the category of cosmos in premodern societies is much indebted to the work of Mircea Eliade.

7. This connection, incidentally, should be taken more seriously by those who are very much in favor of people being able to choose alternative life-styles, while at the same time decrying the alleged materialism of alternative consumer choices in a capitalist economy. But that is another story.

8. Nor is sex-change surgery the only relevant possibility here. As surgery and "genetic engineering" develop further, there is no reason to suppose that the focus will be limited to the sexual organs. The next Promethean venture may entail choices between different possible arrangements of limbs, sense organs, or brain functions. The legal and moral implications of this (not to mention the philosophical ones!) are as yet barely conceivable.

9. For a systematic elaboration of this, see Berger and Luckmann, op. cit., passim.

10. The term "subjectivization" was coined by Arnold Gehlen, and this part of the argument is based on his work. Also, cf. Thomas Luckmann, *The Invisible Religion* (New York: Macmillan, 1967).

11. See Gehlen's "Über die Geburt der Freiheit aus der Entfremdung," in his *Studien zur Anthropologie und Soziologie* (Neuwied/Rhein: Suhrkamp, 1963), pp. 232ff.

12. See Berger, Berger, and Kellner, op. cit., passim.

13. For a systematic elaboration of this, including the relation of secularization and pluralism, see my *The Sacred Canopy*, Part II. For more recent presentations of the problem of secularization, see Rocco Caporale and Antonio Grumelli, eds., *The Culture of Unbelief* (Berkeley: University of California Press, 1971), and Karl-Wilhelm Dahm et al., *Das Jenseits der Gesellschaft* (Munich: Claudius, 1975).

CHAPTER 2

1. In terms of a phenomenological approach to religion, the authors who have influenced me are Rudolf Otto, Gerardus van der Leeuw, and Mircea Eliade. For an overview of this approach, cf. Leeuw's *Religion in Essence and Manifestation* (London: George Allen & Unwin, 1938). Parts of the argument in this chapter, specifically the conceptualization of the supernatural and the sacred, are taken from an article I wrote with Hansfried Kellner, "On the Conceptualization of the Supernatural and the Sacred," *Dialog*, Winter 1978.

2. Cf. Alfred Schutz, "On Multiple Realities," in his *Collected Papers* (The Hague: Nijhoff, 1962), I, 207ff.

3. The phrase "another reality" is, of course, Schutzian. In my opinion, though, the most masterful treatment of this category is to be found in a work of fiction, Robert Musil's great novel *The Man Without Qualities*. I have discussed this in the article "The Problem of Multiple Realities: Alfred Schutz and Robert Musil," in Maurice Natanson, ed., *Phenomenology and Social Reality* (The Hague: Nijhoff, 1970), pp. 213ff. A comparable account (though, I think, less rich than Musil's) is found in the famous episode of the tea-party ecstasy in Proust's *Du côté de chez Swann*. On this, cf. R. C. Zaehner, *Mysticism: Sacred and Profane* (London: Oxford University Press, 1961), pp. 52ff.

4. The term "supernatural" has some unfortunate associations, it hardly needs saying. In terms of recent theology, it is still associated with a violently reactionary and antimodern stance (as in the so-called supernaturalism school of Roman Catholic theology in the nineteenth century). Also, it appears to imply a radical devaluation of the natural world that in its implications might be deemed more Gnostic or Manichaean than Judaeo-Christian. The search for an alternative term therefore suggests itself. My own search has not been successful. "Sacred" will not do, for reasons developed in the present argument. "Transcendent," which I have used elsewhere, is much better, but it has at least as many potentially misleading associations (in this

case, philosophical rather than theological). Here I have settled on "supernatural" once more, *faute de mieux*. I can only hope that a precise delineation of my own use of the term will at least mitigate misunderstanding. The emphasis on "otherness" is, of course, derived from Otto's "*totaliter aliter*," but I differ from Otto in assigning this quality to the supernatural as well as to the sacred.

5. The counterposition of "up above" and "here below" is a recurrent theme in Eliade's work.

6. The predominance of temporal as against spatial symbolism in the Bible has been much made of in recent theology (as, for instance, by Rudolf Bultmann and Oscar Cullman). Thus it is argued by some that the radically temporal, eschatological symbolism of the New Testament ("this aeon" counterposited to "the aeon that is to come") was later "spatialized" by Hellenistically influenced Christian thought. This is, in all likelihood, a correct historical interpretation. My contention is that it must not be elevated to the status of a cognitive criterion. In other words, while it may be quite correct that the Hebrews were obsessed with time and the Greeks with space, the important thing to understand is that *both* symbolizations refer to a transcendence of ordinary space-time reality.

7. In this definition, the key phrase "human attitude" expresses a basic empirical thrust (what, later on in this chapter, is identified with the inductive option). That, of course, is related to my own background as a social scientist, but I don't think that such a background is necessary to accept the usefulness of this definitional starting point. It simply implies that, for purposes of understanding, religion is viewed within an empirical frame of reference, and that, as long as one remains within this frame, religion can only appear as a *human* phenomenon. This does *not* imply that, within a different frame of reference, what first appeared as human may now be seen as a response to more-than-human realities. It may further be said that the proper relation between these two frames of reference is a key problem of any inductive approach to religion that wants to move from empiricism to any sort of theological affirmation. The emphasis on "cosmos" in the definition is derived from Eliade, though Durkheim provides a useful sociological amplification of all that is included in such a "cosmol-

ogy." The term "sacred" is used in Otto's sense, though modified by its counterposition to "supernatural" (as explained).

8. On the definition of mysticism, cf. Zaehner, op. cit.

9. Again, there is a large literature of scholarship demonstrating the nonmystical quality of biblical religion. This demonstration may be accepted *in toto* on the level of historical interpretation without necessarily making this nonmystical quality a cognitive criterion. After all, it *is* possible that the Hebrews missed a couple of things back there!

10. On nonreligious ("profane") mysticism, again cf. Zaehner, op. cit.

11. This description of the sacred is almost completely derived from Rudolf Otto's *The Idea of the Holy*, trans. John W. Harvey (New York: Oxford University Press, 1950).

12. On tradition and institutionalization, cf. Peter L. Berger and Thomas Luckmann, *The Social Construction of Reality* (Garden City, N.Y.: Doubleday, 1966).

13. Sura 97, in *The Koran*, trans. N. J. Dawood (Harmondsworth, Middlesex: Penguin Books, 1956), p. 27.

14. Such anti-institutionalism is characteristic of modern existentialism, which, at least in this respect, stands in a long line of religious radicalisms. I myself tended toward this position in my earlier work both on religion and on society in general (as in *The Precarious Vision*, 1961, and *Invitation to Sociology*, 1963). I would not repudiate altogether what I wrote then on society as "fiction" or on the beatific qualities of individual "ecstasy" and the like. Looking at the world in this way does serve to show (and to "show up") some important features of institutionalized religion and indeed of institutions generally. But it also exaggerates these features and leads to a one-sidedly individualistic (and *ipso facto* less than sociologically adequate) view of human existence.

15. The term is Maurice Halbwachs'. Cf. his *Les cadres sociaux de la mémoire* (Paris: Presses Universitaires de France, 1952).

16. This interpretation is adumbrated in Max Weber's theory of the "routinization of charisma," but it is given a much broader scope here.

17. On symbols, cf. Schutz, op. cit., pp. 287ff.

18. On legitimation, cf. Berger and Luckmann, op. cit., pp. 85ff.

19. Sura 35:24, again in Dawood's translation.

20. *Die fröhliche Wissenschaft*, 125 (Schlechta edition [Munich: Hanser, 1960], II, 127). My translation.

21. Talcott Parsons, *The System of Modern Societies* (Englewood Cliffs, N.J.: Prentice-Hall, 1971).

22. John Murray Cuddihy, *No Offense: Civil Religion and Protestant Taste* (New York: Seabury, 1978). In terms of the social-psychological and cognitive dynamics of pluralism, this book is an important contribution far beyond the particular American phenomena it deals with.

23. Will Herberg, *Protestant—Catholic—Jew* (Garden City, N.Y.: Doubleday, 1955).

24. S. J. Samartha, ed., *Towards World Community: The Colombo Papers* (Geneva: World Council of Churches, 1975), p. 17.

25. Cf. Maurice Natanson, *Edmund Husserl* (Evanston, Ill.: Northwestern University Press, 1973), pp. 42ff.

CHAPTER 3

1. Cf. Karl Barth, *Die protestantische Theologie im 19. Jahrhundert* (Zollikon-Zurich: Evangelischer Verlag, 1952); Horst Stephan and Martin Schmidt, *Geschichte der deutschen evangelischen Theologie* (Berlin: Toepelmann, 1960).

2. Cf. Herbert Hahn, *Old Testament in Modern Research* (Philadelphia: Muhlenberg, 1954).

3. Hans-Joachim Kraus, *Geschichte der historisch-kritischen Erforschung des Alten Testaments* (Neukirchen: Verlag Buchhandlung des Erziehungsvereins, 1956), pp. 236–37.

4. Cf. Stephan and Schmidt, op. cit.; Heinz Zahrnt, *The Question of God: Protestant Theology in the Twentieth Century* (New York: Harcourt, Brace & World, 1969).

5. Cf. Zahrnt, op. cit.

6. Cf. Jürgen Moltmann, ed., *Anfänge der dialektischen Theologie* (Munich: Kaiser, 1962).

7. On the theological aspects of the so-called German Church Struggle during the Nazi period, cf., Heinrich Hermelink, ed., *Kirche im Kampf* (Tübingen: Wunderlich, 1950).

8. Karl Barth, *Kirchliche Dogmatik*, I/1 (Zollikon-Zurich: Evangelischer Verlag, 1947), 10–11. Hereafter cited as *Dogmatik*.

9. This understanding of faith is, of course, at the heart of classical Protestantism. Barth develops it in great detail in his version of the Calvinist doctrine of predestination.

10. It is over this point that Barth broke with his erstwhile ally Emil Brunner. The latter, although quite in accord with the neo-orthodox understanding of revelation, wanted to look for "points of contact" (*Anknüpfungspunkte*) between the revealed Word and man's natural understanding; Barth insisted that there were none.

11. *Dogmatik*, I/1, 26ff. and 73ff.

12. Ibid., pp. 194ff.

13. Ibid., pp. 206ff. The remark on "trembling certainty" is on pp. 237–38.

14. Barth (ibid., p. 231) takes the classical Calvinist statement *Finitum non capax infiniti* ("The finite is not capable of the infinite") and reformulates it: *Homo peccator non capax verbi Domini* ("Sinful man is not capable of the Word of the Lord").

15. Ibid., pp. 239ff.

16. Ibid., p. 250.

17. *Dogmatik*, I/2 (1948), 1. My translation.

18. Ibid., pp. 304ff.

19. Cf. Barth, *Die protestantische Theologie im 19. Jahrhundert*, pp. 484ff.

20. Cf. *Dogmatik*, I/2, pp. 372ff.

21. For a sociology-of-knowledge interpretation of Kierkegaard cf. Michael Plekon, "Kierkegaard: Diagnosis and Disease—An Excavation in Modern Consciousness" (doctoral dissertation, Rutgers University, 1977).

22. Søren Kierkegaard, *Concluding Unscientific Postscript* (Princeton: Princeton University Press, 1941), p. 169.

23. The term "decisionism" was coined by the German sociologist Christian von Krockow. Cf. his *Die Entscheidung* (Stuttgart: Enke, 1958).

24. Cf. Michael Grant, *Jesus* (New York: Scribner's, 1977).

25. Cf. Donald Dawe and John Carman, eds., *Christian Faith in a Religiously Plural World* (Maryknoll, New York: Orbis, 1978), p. 114.

26. Sura 10:99–100, in *The Koran,* trans. N. J. Dawood (Harmondsworth, Middlesex: Penguin Books, 1956), p. 71.

27. Moustafa Mahmoud, *Dialogue avec un ami athée* (Beirut: Dar al-Awda, 1975), p. 217. My translation.

28. It seems appropriate to say here that neo-orthodoxy (in a Lutheran rather than Barthian version) was the theology of my youth, still evident in my first two books. I gradually abandoned this position and by the early 1960s understood myself as a theological liberal. I continue to so understand myself. However, in putting aside an earlier theological position, I am not repudiating or invalidating the experiences that led to that position. In other words, to change one's mind is not to take back one's life!

29. Sura 97 (again in Dawood's translation, p. 27). I have quoted this passage before; it bears repetition! As previously noted, the Arabic word *qadr* means "glory."

30. Cited by R. C. Zaehner, *Mysticism: Sacred and Profane* (London: Oxford University Press, 1961), pp. 157–58.

31. Cf. Nahum Glatzer, *Franz Rosenzweig* (Philadelphia: Jewish Publication Society, 1953).

32. Gretel Weiss has undertaken a sociology-of-knowledge study of this process (doctoral dissertation, Rutgers University, 1978).

33. Cf. Peter L. Berger and Thomas Luckmann, *The Social Construction of Reality* (Garden City, N.Y.: Doubleday, 1966), pp. 144ff.

CHAPTER 4

1. Thomas Altizer and William Hamilton, *Radical Theology and the Death of God* (Indianapolis: Bobbs-Merrill, 1966), p. 11.

2. The primary source for Bultmann's proposal and the ensuing controversy is a series entitled *Kerygma und Mythos*, edited by Hans-Werner Bartsch and published in five volumes between 1948 and 1955 (Hamburg: Reich). Since then, of course, a large literature has grown around the controversy on both sides of the Atlantic, but it cannot be the present purpose to survey this. I reviewed an earlier state of the controversy at the time when it was just beginning to be discussed in this country ("Demythologization: Crisis in Continental Theology," *Review of Religion*, November 1955); the basic features of the issue were quite clear already then. Also, cf. Charles Kegley, ed., *The Theology of Rudolf Bultmann* (New York: Harper & Row, 1966); Walter Schmithals, *An Introduction to the Theology of Rudolf Bultmann* (Minneapolis: Augsburg, 1967). The German word *Entmythologisierung*, incidentally, is as much of an awkward neologism as its English translation.

3. The original essay is to be found in Bartsch, op. cit., I, 15ff.

4. Ibid., p. 18. My translation.

5. This difference is put in German by saying that the New Testament is not interested in *Historie* but in *Geschichte*. The persuasiveness of this distinction, alas, hardly survives translation into any language other than German.

6. Bartsch, op. cit., 50. My translation.

7. Cf. Franz Peerlinck, *Rudolf Bultmann als Prediger* (Hamburg: Reich, 1970).

8. Cf. Peter Berger and Richard Neuhaus, eds., *Against the World for the World* (New York: Seabury, 1976), pp. 8ff.

9. For the former, cf. the criticisms by Julius Schniewind (Bartsch, op. cit., I, 85ff.) and Regin Prenter (ibid., II, 70ff.); for the latter, cf. the criticism of Fritz Buri (ibid., pp. 85ff.).

10. Ibid., III, 9ff.; also, Karl Jaspers and Rudolf Bultmann, *Die Frage der Entmythologisierung* (Munich: Piper, 1954).

11. Karl Barth, *Rudolf Bultmann: Ein Versuch, ihn zu verstehen* (Zollikon-Zurich: Evangelischer Verlag, 1952).

CHAPTER 5

1. The definitive work on Schleiermacher's life and thought continues to be Wilhelm Dilthey's *Leben Schleiermachers* (4 vols., most recently republished by Walter de Gruyter, Berlin, 1966–70). For more recent interpretations, cf. Hugh Mackintosh, *Types of Modern Theology* (New York: Scribner's, 1937), an essentially negative view; Martin Redeker, *Schleiermacher: Life and Thought* (Philadelphia: Fortress, 1973), a balanced vindication of Schleiermacher's theology; Robert Williams: *Schleiermacher the Theologian* (Philadelphia: Fortress, 1978), an interpretation of Schleiermacher in terms of phenomenology that I have found very useful here.

2. Paul Tillich has called this "the Protestant principle."

3. He himself used the term "mystical" for this, but this term is very misleading (and has misled many) if one associates it with the phenomenon commonly called mysticism.

4. Mackintosh (op. cit., p. 86) actually uses the phrase "inductive method." I don't know whether Schleiermacher influenced William James's view that the proper approach to religion should consist of "interpretative and inductive operations" (*The Varieties of Religious Experience* [New York: Collier Books, 1961], p. 339).

5. The sharpest attack on Schleiermacher from this camp was Emil Brunner's *Die Mystik und das Wort* (Tübingen: Mohr, 1924). It is noteworthy that Barth dissociated himself from this one-sidedly pejorative interpretation.

6. *Über die Religion: Reden an die gebildeten unter ihren Verächtern*, in *Sämtliche Werke*, I, (Berlin: Reimer, 1843), 133ff.

7. I use the term "experience" here to translate Schleiermacher's *Gefühl*. I believe that this translation fully meets Schleiermacher's intention and avoids the misunderstandings brought on by translating as "feeling." Cf. Williams, op. cit., pp. 23ff.

8. *Über die Religion*, p. 248. My translation.

9. Ibid., pp. 248–49. The German words here are *Zeichen* and *Andeutungen*.

10. Ibid., p. 249. My translation.

11. Ibid., pp. 316ff. The lecture has the title "On the Social [*das Gesellige*] in Religion." "Church" is defined as "a community [*Gesellschaft*] of human beings whose piety has attained to consciousness" (p. 327). One might amplify this as "*collective* consciousness," and thus move directly from Schleiermacher to Durkheim!

12. Ibid., pp. 385ff., entitled "On the Religions."

13. Ibid., p. 394. My translation.

14. Ibid., p. 403. My translation; my italics. A footnote points out that the term "heresy" was used positively in Hellenistic thought to denote schools of philosophy and medicine, and was also so used to refer to schools in Hellenistic Judaism, and that the pejorative use by Christians is not indicated etymologically.

15. Ibid., p. 247.

16. Schleiermacher may here be compared with the Swedish theologian Anders Nygren, who developed the method of "motif research." This comparison was undertaken by William Johnson: *On Religion: A Study of Theological Method in Schleiermacher and Nygren* (Leiden: Brill, 1964).

17. *Über die Religion*, pp. 433–34. The operative German word here is *Kraft*.

18. *Der christliche Glaube nach den Grundsätzen der evangelischen Kirche*, in *Sämtliche Werke*, vols. III–IV (Berlin: Reimer, 1861).

19. Ibid., III, 6: "*Eine Bestimmtheit des Gefühls oder des unmittelbaren Selbstbewusstseins.*" Again, I believe that *Gefühl* is properly to be translated here as "experience."

20. It is in this sense that Williams (op. cit.) feels entitled to interpret Schleiermacher as a phenomenologist: Consciousness is looked at in terms of what Husserl called its *intentionality*—that is, the object toward which it tends. I agree with this interpretation. In this instance, as Schleiermacher sees it, the object of consciousness is radically metahuman. It is quite erroneous, in consequence, to blame Schleiermacher for Feuerbach's reduction of theology to anthropology.

21. Cf. Horst Stephan and Martin Schmidt, *Geschichte der deutschen evangelischen Theologie* (Berlin: Toepelmann, 1960), pp. 214ff.; Mackintosh, op. cit., pp. 138ff.

22. Cf. Stephan and Schmidt, op. cit., pp. 245ff.; Wilhelm Pauck, *Harnack and Troeltsch* (New York: Oxford University Press, 1968).

23. Adolf Harnack, *Das Wesen des Christentums* (Leipzig: Hinrick, 1905). (Just for curiosity's sake, note that the aristocratic "von" was bestowed upon Harnack at a later date by the Prussian authorities.)

24. In the aforementioned work the word used for experience is *Erleben* (ibid., pp. 93 and 103ff.). I would contend that this usage corresponds to Schleiermacher's *Gefühl*—that is, it refers to the same phenomenon.

25. In the German context, one could say that the Prussian authorities had excellent reasons for bestowing an aristocratic title upon Adolf Harnack!

26. James, op. cit., p. 73.

27. Ibid., p. 34.

28. Ibid., p. 334.

29. Ibid., p. 337.

30. Cf. Pauck, op. cit.; John Clayton, ed., *Ernst Troeltsch and the Future of Theology* (Cambridge: Cambridge University Press, 1976).

31. Ernst Troeltsch, *Die Absolutheit des Christentums* (Tübingen: Mohr, 1912).

32. Ibid., p. 52. My translation.

33. The German words are *Intuition* and *Ahnung* (ibid., p. 73). Troeltsch also says that the absolute is *vorschwebend*; one might translate this freely by saying that the absolute *haunts* the specific religions in their historically relative forms. Whatever the language used, Troeltsch's point is that no group of human beings will ever be the *beati possedentes* of absolute truth.

34. Troeltsch speaks of "a perfectly calm and joyous affirmation of Christianity" (ibid., p. 82; my translation).

35. Troeltsch returned to the problem of the absoluteness of Christianity in the last work of his life, a set of lectures he intended to give in Britain in 1923. These were published posthumously as *Christian Thought: Its History and Application* (London: University of London Press, 1923). While there are differences in emphasis, the basic methodology is unchanged. It should be observed that Troeltsch self-consciously intended to continue Schleiermacher's theological program, above all in his Heidelberg dogmatics lectures of 1911–12. These were also published posthumously, in 1925, under the title *Glaubenslehre* (vol. II of *Gesammelte Schriften* [Aglen, Scientia, 1962]). In these lectures Troeltsch tried to develop a Christian doctrine that would be both a "historical theology" and a "theology of consciousness."

36. An interesting distinction made by Troeltsch is between naïve (= unreflected) and artificial (= theoretical) absoluteness (*Absolutheit des Christentums*, pp. 110ff.). In this, he suggests religion is no different from other human experiences, which undergo a process of transformation as they are reflected and theorized upon. Once such a process has occurred, it is futile to wish to return to the naïve state of unquestioned absoluteness, and the attempts to do so via some theoretical route are artificial and intellectually untenable. In other words, reflection as such is inimical to absoluteness.

37. Ibid., p. 114. My (somewhat free) translation. The word translated as "forces" is *Kräfte*—the plural of *Kraft*, which

Schleiermacher saw as the criterion by which a particular tradition validates itself as revelation and thus becomes scripture.

38. Incidentally, there is the inverse approach—devaluing the insights of "marginal situations" as nothing but the outcome of individual or collective pathology. The present position, of course, is no more compatible with this view than with the view that marginality has a particularly privileged access to truth.

CHAPTER 6

1. This was the position taken by Ernst Troeltsch. One can agree with him on this without thereby agreeing with the details of how he understood the differences between these two religious alternatives.

2. My understanding of this has been greatly influenced by the works of Eric Voegelin and Gerhard von Rad.

3. Rudolf Otto liked to compare the throne vision of Isaiah with the vision of the universal form of Vishnu in the Bhagavad Gita as two prime examples of the experience of the "numinous." Yet the differences are instructive too. Leaving aside the question of the individual in the Hindu scheme of things, the Gita is neither historicizing nor moralizing. History (and indeed the empirical world as a whole) comes to be seen as irrelevant to the religious quest, and in this irrelevance morality becomes relativized. The final practical consequence of the great dialogue between Arjuna and Krishna is that the former overcomes his scruples and goes out into battle against his kinsmen. This fidelity to his caste duty as a warrior is not based on the conviction that this is ultimately right—but that it is ultimately unimportant. To maintain this, it should be strongly emphasized, is *not* to say that those who stand in the tradition of Isaiah have been better people morally than those standing in the tradition of the Gita. It means only that morality has a different religious status in the former tradition as against the latter.

4. That was the view of Heinrich Zimmer, who believed that the practice of Yoga and the Samkhya philosophy were both pre-

Aryan. This view is given credibility by the fact that the Aryan invaders of Iran developed a highly different form of religion. Cf. Zimmer's *Philosophies of India* (Princeton: Princeton University Press, 1951).

5. The researches of Robert Bellah and Charles Glock in the San Francisco area, and their recent elaborations by Robert Wuthnow, are the best empirical evidence on this phenomenon to date. Cf. Bellah and Glock, eds., *The New Religious Consciousness* (Berkeley: University of California Press, 1976); Robert Wuthnow, *Experimentation in American Religion* (Berkeley: University of California Press, 1978).

6. According to public opinion sources, this number runs into millions.

7. Harvey Cox, *Turning East* (New York: Simon & Schuster, 1977); cf. Bellah and Glock, op. cit., as well as several essays in which Bellah shows himself to be more than a sociological observer.

8. Raymond Panikkar, *The Unknown Christ of Hinduism* (London: Darton, Longman & Todd, 1964); John Hick, *God and the Universe of Faiths* (London: Macmillan, 1973); and especially id., *Death and Eternal Life* (Philadelphia: Westminster, 1974), in which Hick is engaged in the fascinating enterprise of trying to reconcile the Indian view of reincarnation with Christianity.

9. Cf. John Hick, ed., *Truth and Dialogue in World Religions* (Philadelphia: Westminster, 1974); Heinrich Dumoulin, *Christianity Meets Buddhism* (LaSalle, Ill.: Open Court, 1974); Donald Dawe and John Carman, eds., *Christian Faith in a Religiously Plural World* (Maryknoll, N.Y.: Orbis, 1978).

10. R. C. Zaehner, *Hindu and Muslim Mysticism* (New York: Schocken, 1969), p. 3.

11. One of the best introductions to mysticism (though the conceptualization leaves something to be desired) is still the chapter on this topic in William James, *The Varieties of Religious Experience* (originally published in 1902; New York: Collier Books, 1961), pp. 299ff. A classical overview is Evelyn Underhill's *Mysticism* (originally published in 1911). On mys-

tical movements in Judaism and Islam respectively, cf. two excellent histories: Gershom Scholem, *Major Trends in Jewish
Mysticism* (New York: Schocken, 1954); and Annemarie
Schimmel, *Mystical Dimensions of Islam* (Chapel Hill: University of North Carolina Press, 1975). For a useful summary
of different theories of mysticism, cf. the first part of Frits
Staal, *Exploring Mysticism* (Berkeley: University of California
Press, 1975); one may profit from this summary without necessarily sharing the author's very negative view of most of
these theories.

12. Cf. Zimmer, op. cit.; also, cf. P. D. Devanandan, *The Concept
of Maya* (Calcutta: YMCA Publication House, 1954); Eliot
Deutsch, *Advaita Vedanta* (Honolulu: East-West Center
Press, 1969).

13. The case of al-Hallaj has been definitively studied by Louis
Massignon, who devoted most of his life to this study, *La
passion d'Al Hosayn Ibn Mansour Al-Hallaj, Martyr mystique
de l'Islam* (Paris, 1922)—published, incidentally, exactly one
thousand years after its subject's execution.

14. James, op. cit., pp. 333–34.

15. Rudolf Otto, *Mysticism East and West* (New York: Macmillan, 1970, first published in 1932).

16. Ibid., p. 14.

17. Zaehner (op. cit.) takes the position that there was significant
direct influence. This is disputed by both Schimmel and Staal
(also in the works cited).

18. Zaehner, op. cit., p. 94. My italics. Zaehner regards this passage
as one very strong piece of evidence for his position regarding
Hindu sources for Sufism.

19. These various interpretations are extensively discussed by
Zaehner, op. cit., passim.

20. Rudolf Otto devoted a book-length study to him: *India's
Religion of Grace and Christianity* (London: Oxford University Press, 1930). Also, cf. R. C. Zaehner, *Mysticism: Sacred
and Profane* (London: Oxford University Press, 1961), pas-

sim.; John Carman, *The Theology of Ramanuja* (New Haven: Yale University Press, 1974).

21. Zaehner, *Mysticism: Sacred and Profane*, especially chapters 8–10.

22. Ibid., p. 172.

23. Ibid., p. 173. My italics.

24. This agenda has in the past been subsumed under the heading of apologetics, in which Christian theology engaged in battles with pantheism and the like. It will be clear by now that I have little sympathy for this type of cognitive warfare. But there is something else wrong with the apologetics approach: It shifts attention from the experiential to the theoretical levels. This, I think, also mars Zaehner's otherwise excellent treatment of these issues, as when he posits the conflict as one between theism and monism. Both of these are theoretical categories by which certain experiences are interpreted. The inductive task is to push past the theoretical superstructures to the underlying experiential roots.

Index

Abraham, 172
  Islam and, 89
Absoluteness, 149
Absoluteness of Christianity, The
  (Troeltsch), 149
Absolutheit des Christentums, Die.
  See Absoluteness of Christianity,
  The
Abstractions, reality and, 39
Abu Yazid, 177–78, 179
Acts, Book of, 79
Adam, 104
Advaita school, 172
Advaita Vedanta (Deutsch), 206
Aesthetic experience, 37ff.
Africa(ns), 23, 187
"Age of Aquarius," 165
Ahura Mazda, 160
Airplane travel, 1–2
Al-Ghazali, 90–91, 148, 178
Al-Hallaj, 173, 177
Alienation, 22ff. *See also* "Death of
  God"; Existentialism
Allah, 85, 86. *See also* Islam and
  Muslims
"Alternative life-styles," 192
Altizer, Thomas, 97, 98
America and Americans, 17, 142, 154,
  171, 186. *See also* specific religions
  Asian religions in, 165–66. *See also*
  specific religions
  and availability of religious
    experience, 36
  and emancipation of Jews, 29
  and eruption of neo-orthodoxy, 71

and ethics; morals, 114, 140
identification of Christianity with
  way of life, 116
as "lead society"; Protestantization,
  58–59
and sexual alternatives, 16
Amida, 78, 179
anathematization, 169
An-atta, 179
Anfänge der dialektischen Theologie,
  197
Angels, 48
Angst, 24, 82, 83, 107, 120. *See also*
  Kierkegaard, Søren
Anknüpfungspunkte, 197
"Another reality," 40–41. *See also*
  Hierophanies; Reality; Sacred, the
"Anthropogenesis," 160
Anthropology, 121, 141–42. *See also*
  Feuerbach, Ludwig
Anti-institutionalism, 48
Anti-Semitism, 29
Anxiety, 107. *See also Angst;* specific
  philosophers
Apologetics, 207
Apostles, 91
  and exorcisms, 103
Arabia. *See also* Arab Nationalism;
  Islam and Muslims
  and hierophany, 89
Arabic language, 50–51, 52
Arab nationalism, 56
Arjuna, 204
Art, modern, 21, 22
Aryans, 163
Ascension, the, 104

Asia. *See* Western Asia; specific
  countries
'Aslama, 85
Atheism, 78. *See also* specific
  philosophers
Athens, 8, 157–58
Atman, 172
Aufhebung (aufgehoben), 78, 79
Authority. *See* Tradition

Baalim, 146
Baghdad, 173
Bali, 1
Bargaining, 98–111
Barrett, Loretta, xv
Barth, Karl (Barthian theory),
  71–79ff., 91ff., 127ff., 136, 151,
  169, 183
  and Brunner's attack on
    Schleiermacher, 200
  Bultmann and, 102, 109, 110, 119
  Protestantische Theologie im 19.
    Jahrhundert, Die, 196
Bartsch, Hans-Werner, 199, 200
Belief, 18ff. *See also* Experience;
  Faith; Mysticism and mystics;
  specific philosophers
  "I believe," 36. *See also* Faith
Bellah, Robert, 166, 205
Benares and Jerusalem, coming
  contestation between, 157–89
Berger, Brigitte, 191, 192
Berger, Peter L., other books by, 191ff.
  See also specific titles
Berlin
  Harnack lectures, 138
  Rosenzweig in, 92
  Schleiermacher lectures, 129
Bhagavad Gita, 204
  and personal devotion, 178
Bhakti, 175, 178
Bible (Scriptures), 42ff., 74ff., 132–33.
  See also New Testament; specific
  books, stories
  and God. *See* God
  language of, 42
  scholarship on, 43, 57, 69–70, 71,
    137, 187. *See also* specific scholars
Birth control, 12–13
Bistam, 177
Bloch, Ernst, 24
Bodhisattvas. *See* Buddhism

Boehme, Jacob, 176
Bourgeoisie, 70–71
Brahman, 172, 175, 179
Brittany and Bretons, 99
Brunner, Emil, 197, 200
Buddhism, 31, 162ff., 169ff., 178, 179
  Pure Land, 78, 179
Bultmann, Rudolf, 102–10ff., 194
Burckhardt, Jacob, 24
Buri, Fritz, 200

Cadres sociaux de la mémoire, Les,
  195
Calvary, 89
Calvinism
  Barth and, 197
  and predestination, 85, 197
  Schleiermacher and, 128
Capitalism, 56, 154, 192
  cause of modernity, 5
  identification of Christianity with,
    116
Caporale, Rocco, 192
Carman, John,
  and *Christian Faith in a Religiously*
    Plural World, 198, 205
  Theology of Ramanuja, The, 207
Caste system, 163
Catholics and Catholicism, 70, 154,
  175–76. *See also* specific
  Catholics, countries
  and modern secularity, 57
  and Protestantization, 58
  and Pure Land Buddhism, 78
  supernaturalism school, 193
Central Europe, 71. *See also* Europe
Certainty, 19, 63, 145–53. *See also*
  Belief; Hierophanies; Inductive
  possibility; Neo-orthodoxy;
  Tradition
Charismatic movement, 171
Childhood, and nostalgia, 67
Choice (choosing), 2–3, 95ff., 132. *See*
  also Modernity
  from fate to, 11–17
Christ. *See* Jesus Christ
Christian Faith, The
  (Schleiermacher), 129, 133–35
Christian Faith in a Religiously Plural
  World, 198, 205
Christianity Meets Buddhism, 205
Christian Thought: Its History and
  Application, 203

Christliche Glaube nach den Grundsätzen den evangelischen Kirche, Der, 201–2
Christocentrism, 77. *See also* Jesus Christ
Church Dogmatics, 73–74. *See also* Barth, Karl
Clayton, John, 202
Clothing, 12
College campuses, and Asian religions, 165
Comic, the (humor), and reality, 39ff.
"Coming back to reality," 38
"Coming home," 67. *See also* Neo-orthodoxy
Communications. *See also* Telephone English language and, 11
Communism, 143
Community (communities), 131, 134. *See also* Sociology
  of consent, 28–29
  and neo-orthodoxy, 92
Comparative religion, 138, 184
Compromises. *See* Bargaining; Inductive possibility
Concept of Maya, The, 206
Concluding Unscientific Postscript, 198
"Condemned to freedom," 23
Confessing Church, 102
Confrontation, 159–61, 168–81
Conscience, throne vision and, 161
Consciousness, 17, 20, 26, 37, 126, 129, 133ff. *See also* Reality
  alterations of, 171
  false, 121
  modern. *See* Modern consciousness
  self-, 133, 135
Conservatism, xiii–xiv, 23. *See also* Tradition
Contestation of religions, 157–89
  "dharma is going West," 158–68
  divinity in confrontation and interiority, 168–81
  waiting for the dark drums of God, 181–89
Contraception, 12–13
Copenhagen, 83
Copernicus, 144
Cosmos and cosmology (universe), 15, 43, 103, 104, 118, 161, 182, 192. *See also* Mythology
Countermodernity, 25

Courage, 18
Cox, Harvey, 166
Crucifixion and the Cross, 104, 109
Cuddihy, John Murray, 58
Cullman, Oscar, 194
Culture of Unbelief, The, 192

Dahm, Karl-Wilhelm, 192
Dawe, Donald, 198, 205
Dawood, N. J., 195, 196, 198
Death, 107. *See also* "Death of God"
  judgment of the dead, 104
  and reality, 40
  souls of the dead, 43
Death and Eternal Life, 205
"Death of God," 55, 97–98
Decision. *See* Choice; Neo-orthodoxy; Reflection
Decisionism, 81, 142
Deductive possibility (deduction), xi, 60, 61–62, 66–94
  case of Protestant neo-orthodoxy, 68–74
  critique of leaping, 79–87
  "flake-like thing on the face of the wilderness," 74–79
  reflecting on thunder, 87–94
Democracy, 140
  Christianity identified with, 116
Demons, 9–10
"Denomination," 58
Dependence, 130
Descartes, René, 20, 21
Destiny. *See* Fate
Deus dixit, 61ff.
Deutsch, Eliot, 206
Devanandan, P. D., 206
Dharma, 165–68
"Dialectical theology," 72, 102. *See also* Barth, Karl; Neo-orthodoxy
Dialog, 193
Dialogue avec un ami athée, 198
Dilthey, Wilhelm, 200
Division of labor, 15
Doppelbödigkeit, 40
Dostoyevsky, Fedor, 23, 70–71, 108
Dreaming, 37ff.
Dressing, 12
Drugs, hallucinatory, 39, 40
Du côté de chez Swann, 193
Dumoulin, Heinrich, 205
Durkheim, Émile, 194

Easter, 89, 107, 109, 110
Eastern Orthodoxy, 58–59
Eckhart, Meister, 174ff.
Ecology, 165
Ecumenicity, x–xi, 158, 159
Edmund Husserl (Natanson), 196
Edwards, Jonathan, 147
Einstein, Albert, 147
Ekstasis, 39
Eliade, Mircea, 88, 150, 192ff.
Elijah, 146
Emerson, Ralph Waldo, 164
"Emissary prophecy," 159
Empiricism, 126, 130, 137, 145, 147,
    148, 182. *See also* Experience;
    specific philosophers
Emptiness, 179ff. *See also* Alienation
English language, 11
Enlightenment, the, 93, 118, 148
    and miracles, 130
    and reductionism, 90
    Schleiermacher and, 128, 130, 148
En-sof, 176
Entmythologisierung, 199
Entscheidung, Die, 198
Epistemology, 20–21
Epistles, Pauline, 71–72, 103
    and derivation of "heresy," 27
*Ernst Troeltsch and the Future of
    Theology*, 202
Eschatology, 109
Essence (*Wesen*), 129–30ff., 136, 138,
    140, 145, 150–51
Essence of Christianity, The, 138
Ethics (morals; morality), 18, 140,
    147, 161, 162, 180
    Jesus' lack of interest in, 145
    and translation model, 113–15
Europe (European culture), 23,
    70–71. *See also* specific countries,
    philosophers
    and emancipation of Jews, 29
    and technological revolution, 4–5
Existentialism, 24, 81, 82, 95, 106–7ff.,
    118, 151, 182. *See also* Alienation;
    specific philosophers
Exodus, Book of, 76
Exorcisms, 103
Experience, 32ff., 46ff., 75–76. *See also*
    Deductive possibility; Inductive
    possibility; Reflection
    religion as, 41–46ff.
Experimentation in American

Religion, 205
Exploring Mysticism, 206
Extramarital sex. *See* Sex and
    sexuality
Exxon Education Foundation, xv

Faith, 74ff., 92, 107ff., 129, 131, 135,
    141, 152. *See also* Belief; specific
    philosophers
    "leap of faith," 80ff., 94, 108, 181
False consciousness, 121
Fana, 177, 178
Fanaticism, 155, 182
Fate, 11–17ff. *See also* Tradition
Feminism, 16
Fertility gods, 160
Feuerbach, Ludwig, 52, 78, 121–24
    Schleiermacher and, 130, 202
"Finite provinces of meaning," 37
Finitum non capax infiniti, 197
First World War. *See* World War I
Frage der Entmythologisierung, Die,
    200
France (the French), study of impact
    of urban life on religion in, 98–99
Franz Rosenzweig (Glatzer), 198
Freud, Sigmund (Freudian theory),
    78, 122, 183
    and projection, 52
    and repression, 121
Fröhliche Wissenschaft, Die, 196

Galatians, Epistle to the, 27
Galilee, 53, 89
Gandhi, Mohandas K., 164
Gare du Nord (Paris), 99
Garuda (airline), 1
Gay movement, 16
Gehlen, Arnold, 192
"Genetic engineering," 192
German Church Struggle, 197
Germany and Germans, 71, 72–73,
    80ff., 91–92, 101–2, 109, 136, 155.
    See also Nazism; specific Germans
    Thirty Years' War, 180
*Geschichte der deutschen
    evangelischen Theologie*, 196, 202
Ghetto, 29
Glatzer, Nahum, 198
Glaubenslehre (Troeltsch), 203
Glock, Charles, 205
Gnosticism, 163
    "supernatural" and, 193

God, 144, 159ff., 169ff., 175, 176, 178, 180, 182, 188. *See also* specific philosophers, religions
"death of," 55, 97–98
and deductive possibility, 61, 74ff.
and inductive possibility, 130, 131, 134, 146ff., 156
and reductive possibility, 104, 106, 109, 112, 116, 118
Word of, 74ff.
God and the Universe of Faiths, 205
Godhead, 175–76
Gods, 96. *See also* Mythology
as symbols, 123
Goethe, Johann Wolfgang von, 164
Gospels, the, 103. *See also* New Testament
Grace, 74, 76, 108
"religion of," 78
Grant, Michael, 198
Gravity, 14
Greeks (and Hellenism), 24, 161, 187, 201
and fate, 14
Indian influence on mystery cults in, 163
vs. Jerusalem, 157–58
and space, 194
Greene, William, 191
Greifswald, University of, 69
Grumelli, Antonio, 192
Guatemala, 187
Guevara, Che, 116

Hahn, Herbert, 196
Hairein, 27
Halbwachs, Maurice, 195
Hallucination (hallucinatory drugs), 39, 40
Hamilton, William, 199
Harnack, Adolf von, 137–38, 140, 141, 151
and 1914 war hysteria, 143
Harnack and Troeltsch, 202
Hartford Appeal, xiii–xiv
Harvey, John W., 195
Heber, Reginald, 59
Hebrews. *See* Jews and Judaism
Hegel, Georg Wilhelm Friedrich (Hegelian theory), 149, 183
and historicizing, 126
Heidegger, Martin (Heideggerian theory), 106, 107, 120

Heidelberg, 203
Hellenism. *See* Greeks
Herberg, Will, 58
Heresy, 132, 171
Heretical imperative, 26–31. *See also* Inductive possibility
Hermelink, Heinrich, 197
Hick, John, 166
Hierophanies, 88–91, 150, 153, 161. *See also* specific events, writers
Hindu and Muslim Mysticism (Zaehner), 205, 206
Hinduism and Hindus, 60, 84, 162ff., 169–70ff.
Barth and, 84
Bhagavad Gita, 178, 204
"Historism"; "historicizing," 126ff., 161. *See also* Inductive possibility
History (historical science), 43, 53, 122, 126ff., 136–39, 144–45, 146, 149–50, 153, 161, 162, 169, 185. *See also* Bible
Holy Scriptures. *See* Bible
Holy Spirit, 103, 104
"Homecoming" ("coming home"), 67. *See also* Neo-orthodoxy
Homeless Mind, The (Berger, Berger, and Kellner), 191, 192
Homosexuality, the gay movement, 16
Honor, 18
Humanism. *See* Ethics
Humor (the comic), and reality, 39ff.
Husserl, Edmund, 64, 202

"I am truth," 173
"Ideal types," 61
Idea of the Holy, The, 195
Identity, 13, 14
Illusion, 175, 179
Images, 125
"immediate self-consciousness," 133
Imperialism, 163–64
India, xi, 60, 84, 89, 150. *See also* Hindus and Hinduism
and coming contestation of religions between Jerusalem and Benares, 157–89
India's Religion of Grace and Christianity, 206
Indonesia, national airline of, 1
Indra, 162–63
Inductive possibility (induction), xi, 60, 62–65, 69, 125–56, 170, 181ff.

See also specific philosophers
back to Schleiermacher, 127–35
in defense of mellowness, 153–56
inductive model, 135–39
criticisms of, 139–45
quest for certainty and its
frustration, 145–53
Indus civilization, 162
Industrial revolution, 56
Infinite, the, 130. *See also* Essence;
Mysticism and mystics
"Infinity, mysticism of," 172–73ff.
Insanity, mysticism and, 147
Insights, 155–56
Institutions, 13ff. *See also* Pluralism;
Tradition
Interiority, 161ff., 168–81
*Introduction to the Theology of
Rudolf Bultmann, An,* 199
Invisible Region, The, 192
Invitation to Sociology, 195
Iran, 168
Aryan invaders, 205
dualism of, 163
and hierophany, 89
Isaac, 172
Isaiah, 161, 170, 173
Isaiah, Book of, 161
Ishvara, 175
Islam and Muslims, 31, 48, 51, 56, 66
85–86, 161, 163, 169, 173, 176–77,
186. *See also* Koran; Muhammad
Al-Ghazali on mystics, 90–91
and *Church Dogmatics,* 84–85
Israel, 137, 146. *See also* Bible;
Jerusalem; Jews and Judaism

Jacob, 172
Jainism, 162, 172
James, William, 146–47, 173, 180, 200,
205
and "accent of reality," 38
and "infallible credentials," 151
and "subuniverses," 37
Japan (Japanese), 164
Pure Land Buddhism, 78, 179
Jaspers, Karl, 117–18, 120
and "marginal situations," 155
Jenseits der Gesellschaft, Das, 192
Jerusalem, 53, 89
and Benares, coming contestation
between, 157–89

Jesus (Grant), 198
Jesus Christ, 53, 77, 89, 104, 106ff.,
110, 112ff., 116, 134, 135, 144,
145, 159, 169, 172. *See also* New
Testament; Resurrection
and exorcisms, 103
and loaves and fishes, 100
as mediator, 132
Satan urges jump off Temple, 108
Jet travel, 1–2
Jews and Judaism (Hebrews;
Israelites), 31, 44, 114, 145, 154,
157, 159ff., 167, 169, 170, 173,
186. *See also* Bible; Israel; Moses
emancipation of, 29–30
Hellenistic, 201
and manna from Heaven, 76, 85
and neo-orthodoxy, 91–92
"Protestantization" in America, 58
Schleiermacher and "stunted"
character of, 132
and time, 194
John, Gospel of, 157
Johnson, William, 201
Jokes, and reality, 39
Joseph, Brother, 180
Judaism. *See* Jews and Judaism
Judgment of the dead, 104
Junayd, 177–78, 179
Jungians, 115

Kant, Immanuel, 128–29
Karma, 162
Kegley, Charles, 199
Kellner, Hansfried, xv, 191ff.
Kerygma, 75, 84, 93, 103, 106ff. *See
also* Revelation
Kerygma und Mythos (Bartsch, ed.),
199, 200
Kierkegaard, Søren, 23, 70–71, 80ff.,
107, 108, 143, 144
Mynster and, 24
Kirche im Kampf, 197
Kirchliche Dogmatik. See Barth, Karl
"Knight of faith," 81
Koran, 48, 54, 85–86, 89–90, 169, 172
language of, 50–51, 52
Kraus, Hans-Joachim, 196
Krishna, 204
Krockow, Christian von, 198
Kulturprotestantismus, 142–43

Index

Lagos, 23
Language, 50–51. *See also* Translation
English, 11
Latin America, 116
"Lead society," 58
Leaping ("leap of faith"), 79–87, 94, 108, 181
Leben Schleiermachers, 200
LeBras, Gabriel, 98–99
Leeuw, Gerardus van der, 193
Left, the, xiv, 115, 154. *See also* Liberalism; Revolutionism
Legitimation, 15, 52, 55, 143. *See also* Experience; Reflection
Levy, Marion, 3, 4
Liberalism, xii, xiv, 136ff., 149ff., 182–83. *See also* Bultmann, Rudolf; Deductive possibility; Inductive possibility; Schleiermacher, Friedrich
Liberalism, and bargaining, 101ff.
Liberation, 22ff. *See also* Choice
Literature, modern, 21, 22
"Living toward death," 107
Loaves and fishes, miracle of the, 100
Logos, 157
Lotus position, 162
Love, 43
Loyalty, 18
Lubavitcher Hassidism, 30
Luckmann, Thomas
Invisible Religion, 192
and *Social Construction of Reality,* 191, 192, 195, 196, 199
Luria, Isaac, 176
Luther, Martin, 107, 128, 171
"heart bent back upon itself," 107
"Here I stand . . . ," 105
Lutheran(ism), xiii, 73, 198. *See also* Reformation; specific Lutherans

Mackintosh, Hugh, 200
Madness, mysticism and, 147
Magicians, 44
Mahayana, 78, 179
Mahmoud, Moustafa, 198
Major Trends in Jewish Mysticism, 206
Manichaeanism, 193
"Manifesto of the Intellectuals," 72
Manna from heaven, 76, 85
Man Nobody Knows, The, 116

Man Without Qualities, The, 193
Marburg, University of, 102
"Marginal situations," 155–56
Marriage, and pluralization, 16
Marx, Karl (Marxism), 25, 52, 78, 115, 122, 164, 183
and false consciousness, 121
Maslow, Abraham, 115
Massignon, Louis, 206
Mathematics, pure, and reality, 39
Maya. See Illusion
Meditation, 85, 132, 165. *See also* specific philosophers
Mellowness, 153–56, 187
Memory. *See* Nostalgia; Tradition
Mental health. *See* Psychology
Messiah, 157
Methodism, 171
Migration, and impact of urban life on religion, 99
Military institutions (soldiers), 18–19
Miracles, 130. *See also* specific miracles
Mi'raj, 178
Missionaries, 59–60, 163–67, 169
and Pure Land Buddhism, 78
Missionswissenschaft, 167
Modern consciousness, 5ff., 96ff., 154. *See also* Modernity; Reductive possibility
Modernity (modernization), 1–31, 54–56ff., 63, 126, 176, 183ff. *See also* Reductive possibility
bargaining with, 98–100ff.
and deductive possibility, 66ff., 80–81ff., 87
from fate to choice, 11–17
heretical imperative, 26–31
and inductive possibility, 126. *See also* Inductive possibility; specific philosophers
modern man as nervous Prometheus, 22–26
plurality of worldviews, 17–22
Western imperialism and, 164
Modernization: Latecomers and Survivors, 191
Moira, 14
Moira: Fate, Good and Evil in Greek Thought, 191
Moltmann, Jürgen, 197

Monotheism, 159. *See also* specific
   religions
Morals. *See* Ethics
Moses, 89, 172
   and manna, 76
"Motif research," 201
Mount Carmel, 146
Muhammad, 48, 66, 86, 89, 90, 159,
   172
   and language, 51, 52
"Multiple realities," 37
Music, listening to, 37ff.
Musil, Robert, 193
Muslims. *See* Islam and Muslims
Mynster, Bishop, 24
Mystery cults, Greek, 163
Mystical Dimensions of Islam, 206
Mysticism (Underhill), 205
Mysticism and mystics, 33–34, 44–45,
   47, 90–91, 163, 168–81
   "of infinity," 172–73ff.
   "of personality," 171–72ff.
   and time, 152
   William James and, 147–48
Mysticism East and West, 206
Mysticism: Sacred and Profane
   (Zaehner), 193, 195, 198, 206–7
Mystik und das Wort, Die, 200
Mythology, 9–10, 14
   bargaining away, 101–10ff.

Nairobi, 23
Natanson, Maurice, 193, 196
Nation-state
   and modernity, 5
   as sacred, 46
"Nativism," 67
Nature cults, 160
Nazism, 155
   Barth, Barthian theology and, 72,
      73, 143
   Bultmann and, 102
   and "myth of the twentieth
      century," 105
Near East, 160. *See also* specific
   countries
Necessity, 14–15
Neo-orthodoxy, xii, 67–74, 79ff.,
   91–94, 97, 100, 129, 136, 137, 139,
   141, 144, 154, 155, 182. *See also*
   Barth, Karl; Deductive possibility
"Neotraditionalism," 67, 68
Neuhaus, Richard, 199

New Religious Consciousness, The,
   205
New Testament, 53, 79, 145, 188. *See
   also* Gospels; specific books,
   scholars
   and appearance of existentialism in
      history, 108
   and derivation of "heresy," 27
   and mythological worldview, 103ff.
   and temporal/spatial symbolism,
      194
"New Testament and Mythology," 102
Niebuhr, Richard, 58
Nietzsche, Friedrich, 23, 70–71, 122
   Burckhardt and, 24
   and "death of God," 55, 97, 98
"Night of Glory" (Qadr), 48, 85, 89
Nihilation, 169ff.
Niles, D. T., 84
Nostalgia, 24–25, 64, 160
Novel, the, 21
Nygren, Anders, 201

Objectivity, 13–15, 21, 81, 82. *See also*
   Reality; Tradition
Occultist movements, 105
Old Testament in Modern Research,
   196
On Religion (Johnson), 201
On Religion (Schleiermacher), 129–33
Open-mindedness, 63. *See also*
   Inductive possibility
Orgasm, and reality, 39
Orthodox Church, 58–59
Orthodoxy, 97, 130, 135, 137, 141, 143,
   144. *See also* Neo-orthodoxy;
   Tradition
Other reality; otherness, 40–41. *See
   also* Hierophanies; Reality;
   Sacred, the
Otto, Rudolf, 45, 139, 148, 193
   study of Eckhart and Shankara, 174,
      175

Pacifism, and ethics, 114
Pain
   and plausibility, 18
   and reality, 39
Palestine, 89. *See also* Israel
Panikkar, Raymond, 166
Pannenberg, Wolfhart, 139
Pantheism, 207
Paramount reality, 37–41

Parapsychology, 44
Paris, 99
Parsons, Talcott, 58
Particularism, 77ff.
Pascal, Gabriel, 10
*Passion d'Al Hosayn Ibn Mansour
Al-Hallaj, Martyr mystique de
l'Islam, La,* 206
Pauck, Wilhelm, 202
Paul, St. (and epistles), 100, 103
    Barth's book on Epistle to Romans,
    71–72
    and derivation of "heresy," 27
Payton, Robert, xv
Peale, Norman Vincent, 115
Peerlinck, Franz, 199
Pentateuch, 69
Pentecost, 89, 103
"Personality, mysticism of," 171–72ff.
Phenomenology, 37, 131–33. *See also*
    Reality
Phenomenology and Social Reality,
    193
Philosophies of India (Zimmer), 205,
    206
Philosophy, 18, 20–21ff., 119, 123, 182.
    See also specific philosophers
Physics, abstract, and reality, 39
Pietism, 128
Piety, 153, 175. *See also* specific
    philosophers, religions
"Pious communities," 134
Pius XI, 65
Plausibility, 17ff., 47–48, 54, 62, 63, 67,
    72–73, 82ff., 98ff., 154–55, 183. *See
    also* Pluralism; Reality;
    Secularism; Tradition
Pleasure, and reality, 39
Plekhan, Michael, 198
Pluralism (pluralization; plurality), 5,
    15–22ff., 83, 120, 131, 154, 186
    and worldviews, 17–22
"Points of contact," 197
Politics (political theory), 121, 143
    and language, 115–16
Polo, Marco, 123
Possession, 103
Power
    and modernity, 3
    and projection, 52
Pragmatism. *See* James, William
Preachers and preaching, 74, 109, 137,
    151

Precarious Vision, The, 195
Predestination, 197
Pregnancy, and birth control, 12–13
Prenter, Regin, 200
"Professional theologians," xiii
Projection, 52, 78, 121–24
Prometheus, modern man as a
    nervous, 22–26
Prophets, 152, 159ff.
    Isaiah, 161, 170, 173
Protestant—Catholic—Jew, 196
"Protestant era," 58
*Protestantische Theologie im 19.
    Jahrhundert, Die,* 196, 197
Protestantism, xii, 33, 101ff., 126–27,
    128, 135ff. *See also* Liberalism;
    Neo-orthodoxy; Reformation;
    specific Protestants
    assorted miseries of, 56–60
    and "death of God," 55, 97–98
"Protestantization," 58–59
"Protestant principle," 200
Proust, Marcel, 193
"Psychologism," 142
Psychology (psychological sciences),
    21, 22, 115, 116, 121, 122
Pure Land Buddhism, 78, 179

Qadr, Night of, 48, 85, 89
Quasi mysticism, 171–72
Question of God (Zahrnt), 196, 197
Qushayri, 177, 178

Racial tolerance, and ethics, 115
Rad, Gerhard von, 204
*Radical Theology and the Death of
    God,* 199
Ramanuja, 178–79
Ranke, Leopold von, 126, 144
Reactionary ideologies. *See* Nostalgia
Reaffirmation. *See* Deductive
    possibility; Neo-orthodoxy
Reality, 36–41. *See also* Sacred, the;
    Supernatural
Reasonableness. *See* Inductive
    possibility
Redeker, Martin, 200
Redemption. *See* Salvation
Reductionism, 64, 90, 140. *See also*
    Reductive possibility
Reductive possibility (reduction), xi,
    60, 62, 95–124
    bargaining away mythology, 101–10

bargaining with modernity, 98–101
man as symbolizer and symbol, 121–24
translation model, 110–17
critique of, 117–21
Reflection, 20, 21, 33–34, 52–54, 55, 63, 64, 69, 74, 81, 98, 130, 141, 181, 182. *See also* specific philosophers, possibilities
reflecting on thunder, 87–94
Reformation (Protestant), 5, 56, 127, 128
as "conspiracy of the junior faculty," 188
Reincarnation, 162, 205
Relativity (relativization), 10, 24, 39, 53–54, 87, 149, 153
theory of, 147
Religion in Essence and Manifestation, 193
"Religious preference," 17, 30
"Religious virtuosi," 33–34, 147
Renaissance, the, 5
Repression, Freudian theory of, 121
Resurrection, 100, 104. *See also* Easter
Revelation, 130–31, 141. *See also* Neo-orthodoxy; Prophets; Word of God
Review of Religion, 199
"Revivalism," 67, 128, 171
Revolutionism (revolutionary movements), 23, 25, 64, 155
as sacred, 46
Richelieu, Armand Jean du Plessis, Cardinal, 180
Right, the, xiv, 115–16, 154. *See also* Secularism
Ritschl, Albrecht, 137, 140, 141
Roman Catholics. *See* Catholics and Catholicism
Romans, Epistle to the, 71–72
Romantic movement, 128
Rosenzweig, Franz, 91–92
"Routinization of charisma," 195
Rudolf Bultmann: Ein Versuch, ihn zu verstehen, 200
Rudolf Bultmann als Prediger, 199
Rumor of Angels, A, ix–x
Russian Orthodox Church, 59
Rutgers University, xv
Ruysbroeck, John, 180

Sacred, the, 41ff., 55, 154, 193. *See also* Hierophanies; Mythology; specific religions
Sacred Canopy, The, 192
Saints, 162–63, 180
Teresa of Avila, 147, 148, 180
Salvation, 78, 79, 89, 104, 134, 162
Samartha, S. J., 196
Samkhya Yoga, 172, 204–5
Samsara-karma, 162
San Francisco, 205
Sartre, Jean-Paul, 23, 107
Camus vs., 24
Satan, 108
Schelling, Friedrich Wilhelm Joseph, 128
Schimmel, Annemarie, 206
Schleiermacher, Friedrich, xii, 64–65, 68–69, 83, 101, 127–36ff., 148, 151, 182
Schleiermacher: Life and Thought, 200
Schleiermacher the Theologian (Williams), 200ff.
Schmidt, Martin, 196, 202
Schmithals, Walter, 199
Schniewind, Julius, 200
Scholasticism, 187
Scholem, Gershom, 206
Schopenhauer, Arthur, 164
Schutz, Alfred, 37–39, 193, 196
and "standard time," 152
Science, 105, 123, 182
Jaspers criticizes Bultmann on, 119
as sacred, 46
"Scientism," 119
Scriptures. *See* Bible
Second Vatican Council, 57
Second World War. *See* World War II
Secretariat for the Non-Christian Religions, 166
Sectarianism, neo-orthodoxy and, 92
Sects, 92
Secularism (secularization), xii, xiv, 26, 27, 96, 99ff., 108, 109, 111ff., 140, 154, 155, 166, 182ff., 189. *See also* Modernity
Self-consciousness, 133, 135
Sense of humor. *See* Humor
Sex and sexuality, 160, 168–69
and birth control, 12
and ethics, 114
orgasm and reality, 39

and pluralization, 15–16
and projection, 52
Sex-change surgery, 16
"Sexual life-style," 16
Shankara, 174–75ff.
Shirk, 85
Shiva, 178
Shunyata, 179, 180
Silesius, Angelus, 176
Sin, 104
  Paul and sinners, 100
Situation, 5–6ff. *See also*
  Existentialism; Modernity
Sitz im Leben, 122
Sivaraman, K., 59–60
Slavery, Paul and, 100
Sleep. *See* Dreaming
Social Construction of Reality, The,
  191, 192, 196, 199
Social sciences, 53, 122, 185
Society (social entities), 17ff., 43, 48,
  49. *See also* Institutions;
  Modernity; Tradition
  and being "alone," 55
  and paramount reality, 38
Sociology, 22, 23, 116–17, 120–21, 131,
  143
Sociology of Knowledge, The, 191
Socrates, 8
Soldiers (the military), 18–19
Sorge, 107
Souls, 43
Space, the supernatural and, 42–43
Staal, Frits, 206
Standortsgebundenheit, 191
Stark, Werner, 191
Stephan, Horst, 196, 202
*Studien zur Anthropologie und
  Soziologie*, 192
Subjectivity (subjectivization), 18,
  20–21, 67, 69, 81, 82, 126, 128,
  133. *See also* Deductive possibility
"Subuniverses," 37
"Suffering servant," 68
Sufis (Sufism), 91, 176ff.
Supernatural, 41ff., 152, 154, 193. *See
  also* Mythology
"Supernaturalism," 193
Surgery, 16
Symbols (symbolization), 50ff.,
  121–24. *See also* specific writers
Syria-Palestine, and hierophanies, 89
System of Modern Societies, The, 196

Taxes, 15
Technology, 4ff., 24
Telephone, 6–7, 11
Teresa of Avila, St., 147, 148, 180
Tertullian, 157, 158
"Theological Declaration of Barmen,"
  72
Theology of Ramanuja, The, 207
Theology of Rudolf Bultmann, The,
  199
Thinking. *See* Reflection
Third World, x, 6–7, 12, 164. *See also*
  Western Asia; specific countries
  and ambivalence of alienation and
    liberation, 23
  birth control in, 12–13
  jet travel in, 1–2
  and telephones, 6
Thirty Years' War, 180
Thought. *See* Reflection
"Three-story universe," 103
Throne vision, 161, 173
Tikal, 187
Tillich, Paul, 139, 186
  "Protestant era," 58
  "Protestant principle," 200
Time, supernatural and, 42–43
Tools, 11–12
Torah, 169, 172
Totalitarianism, 25–26
Totaliter aliter, 45
Towards World Community, 196
Tradition, 12ff., 19, 23ff., 32ff., 57,
  62ff., 181, 184. *See also* Deductive
    possibility; Inductive possibility;
    Institutions; Neo-orthodoxy
  modernizing. *See* Reductive
    possibility
  religion as, 46–54
Transcendence. *See* Hierophanies;
  Mythology; Supernatural
Translation (translation model),
  112–21
  critique of model, 117–21
"Trembling certainty," 76
Troeltsch, Ernst, 149–53, 187, 204
"True self," 43
Truth, 94. *See also* Certainty; Faith
*Truth and Dialogue in World
  Religions*, 205
Turkey, 67
Turning East, 205

Types (typology), 60–61, 168
Types of Modern Theology, 200

Über die Religion. See On Religion (Schleiermacher)
Underhill, Evelyn, 205
Universe. *See* Cosmos and cosmology
Unknown Christ of Hinduism, The, 205
Upanishads, 172, 177, 185
Shankara and, 174–75
Urban life (French), impact on religion of, 98–99

Values. *See* Subjectivity
Varieties of Religious Experience (James), 146–48, 200, 205, 206
Vatican
and Asian religions, 166
Council, Second, 57
Vedanta, 172, 174
Vishnu, 178, 204
Voegelin, Eric, 204

War. *See also* specific wars
and ethics, 115
Weber, Max (Weberian theory), 33, 147, 149, 168
"emissary prophecy," 159
and "ideal types," 61
and Protestant Reformation, 56
and "routinization of charisma," 195
Weiss, Gretel, 198
Wellhausen, Julius, 69–70
Wesen. See Essence
Wesen des Christentums, Das. See Essence of Christianity, The
Wesley, John, 171
Western Asia, xi, 88–89, 150
coming contestation of religions between Jerusalem and Benares, 157–89

Western civilization (Western culture; the West), 21–22, 31, 33, 97, 140, 158
and development of Protestantism, 56
imperialism, 163–64
and missionaries. *See* Missionaries
philosophy since Descartes, 20–21
Will. *See* Choice; Neo-orthodoxy
Williams, Robert, 200ff.
Women, Paul and, 100
Word of God, 74ff.
World Council of Churches, 59–60
and Asian religions, 166
Worldviews, 10. *See also* Mythology; specific philosophers, possibilities
modernity and. *See* Modernity
plurality of, 17–22
World War I (First World War), 70ff., 128, 143
World War II (Second World War), 71, 73, 139
Bultmann and, 102
Worth, Robert, 205

Yahweh (Yahwism), 146, 160
Yoga, 162
Samkhya, 172, 204–5
Yom Kippur, 92
"You are that," 172, 177
Youth, and nostalgia, 67

Zaehner, R. C., 179–81
Hindu and Muslim Mysticism, 205, 206
Mysticism: Sacred and Profane, 193, 195, 198, 206–7
Zahrnt, Heinz, 196, 197
Zimmer, Heinrich, 204–5, 206
Zoroaster, 159, 160, 168
Zwischen den Zeiten, 72